POETRY FROM CRESCENT MOON

William Shakespeare: *Selected Sonnets and Verse*
edited, with an introduction by Mark Tuley

William Shakespeare: *Complete Poetry*
edited and introduced by Mark Tuley

*Shakespeare: Love, Poetry and Magic
in Shakespeare's Sonnets and Plays*
by B.D. Barnacle

Edmund Spenser: *Heavenly Love: Selected Poems*
selected and introduced by Teresa Page

Robert Herrick: *Delight In Disorder: Selected Poems*
edited and introduced by M.K. Pace

Sir Thomas Wyatt: *Love For Love: Selected Poems*
selected and introduced by Louise Cooper

John Donne: *Air and Angels: Selected Poems*
selected and introduced by A.H. Ninham

D.H. Lawrence: *Being Alive: Selected Poems*
edited with an introduction by Margaret Elvy

D.H. Lawrence: Symbolic Landscapes
by Jane Foster

D.H. Lawrence: Infinite Sensual Violence
by M.K. Pace

Percy Bysshe Shelley: *Paradise of Golden Lights: Selected Poems*
selected and introduced by Charlotte Greene

Thomas Hardy: *Her Haunting Ground: Selected Poems*
edited, with an introduction by A.H. Ninham

Sexing Hardy: Thomas Hardy and Feminism
by Margaret Elvy

Emily Bronte: *Darkness and Glory: Selected Poems*
selected and introduced by Miriam Chalk

John Keats: *Bright Star: Selected Poems*
edited with an introduction by Miriam Chalk

Henry Vaughan: *A Great Ring of Pure and Endless Light: Selected Poems*
selected and introduced by A.H. Ninham

The Crescent Moon Book of Love Poetry
edited by Louise Cooper

The Crescent Moon Book of Mystical Poetry in English
edited by Carol Appleby

The Crescent Moon Book of Nature Poetry From Langland to Lawrence
edited by Margaret Elvy

The Crescent Moon Book of Metaphysical Poetry
edited and introduced by Charlotte Greene

The Crescent Moon Book of Elizabethan Love Poetry
edited and introduced by Carol Appleby

The Crescent Moon Book of Romantic Poetry
edited and introduced by L.M. Poole

Blinded By Her Light The Love-Poetry of Robert Graves
by Jeremy Mark Robinson

The Best of Peter Redgrove's Poetry: The Book of Wonders
by Peter Redgrove, edited and introduced by Jeremy Mark Robinson

Peter Redgrove: Here Comes the Flood
by Jeremy Mark Robinson

Sex-Magic-Poetry-Cornwall: A Flood of Poems
by Peter Redgrove, edited with an essay by Jeremy Mark Robinson

Brigitte's Blue Heart
by Jeremy Reed

Claudia Schiffer's Red Shoes
by Jeremy Reed

By-Blows: Uncollected Poems
by D.J. Enright

Petrarch, Dante and the Troubadours: The Religion of Love and Poetry
by Cassidy Hughes

Dante: *Selections From the Vita Nuova*
translated by Thomas Okey

Arthur Rimbaud: *Selected Poems*
edited and translated by Andrew Jary

Elizabethan Sonnet Cycles

ELIZABETHAN SONNET CYCLES

Five Major Elizabethan Sonnet Sequences

by

Samuel Daniel, Michael Drayton, Sir Philip Sidney, William Shakespeare and Edmund Spenser

Edited by Mark Tuley

CRESCENT MOON

CRESCENT MOON PUBLISHING
P.O. Box 1312, Maidstone,
Kent, ME14 5XU
Great Britain, www.crmoon.com

First published 2013.

Printed and bound in North America.
Set in Garamond Book 11 on 14pt.
Designed by Radiance Graphics.

The right of Mark Tuley to be identified as the editor of this book has been
asserted generally in accordance with sections 77 and 78 of the Copyright,
Designs and Patents Act 1988.

British Library Cataloguing in Publication data

ISBN-13 9781861712745 (Pbk)
ISBN-13 9781861714473 (Hbk)

CONTENTS

Sir Philip Sidney, National Portrait Gallery, London

Sir Philip Sidney

Samuel Daniel

Michael Drayton

Edmund Spenser

William Shakespeare

William Shakespeare, by Eric Gill, 1936

London around 1600

Astrophel and Stella

SIR PHILIP SIDNEY

(1554-1586)

I

Louing in trueth, and fayne in verse my love to show,
  That she, deare Shee, might take som pleasure of my
                     paine,
Pleasure might cause her reade, reading might make her
                     know,
  Knowledge might pittie winne, and pity grace obtaine,
I sought fit wordes to paint the blackest face of woe;
  Studying inuentions fine, her wits to entertaine,
Oft turning others leaues, to see if thence would flow
  Some fresh and fruitfull showers upon my sun-burnd
                     brain.
But words came halting forth, wanting Inuentions stay;
  Inuention, Natures childe, fledde step-dame Studies
                     blowes;
And others feet still seemde but strangers in my way.
  Thus, great with childe to speak, and helplesse in my
                     throwes,
    Biting my trewand pen, beating myselfe for spite,
    Fool, said my Muse to me, looke in thy heart, and write.

II

Not at the first sight, nor with a dribbed shot,
   Love gaue the wound, which, while I breathe, will bleede;
But knowne worth did in tract of time proceed,
   Till by degrees, it had full conquest got.
I saw and lik'd; I lik'd but loved not;
   I lov'd, but straight did not what Love decreed:
At length, to Loves decrees I, forc'd, agreed,
   Yet with repining at so partiall lot.
Now, euen that footstep of lost libertie
   Is gone; and now, like slaue-borne Muscouite,
I call it praise to suffer tyrannie;
    And nowe imploy the remnant of my wit
      To make myselfe beleeue that all is well,
      While, with a feeling skill, I paint my hell.

III

Let dainty wits crie on the Sisters nine,
    That, brauely maskt, their fancies may be told;
Or, Pindars apes, flaunt they in phrases fine,
    Enam'ling with pied flowers their thoughts of gold;
Or else let them in statlier glorie shine,
    Ennobling new-found tropes with problemes old;
Or with strange similes enrich each line,
    Of herbes or beasts which Inde or Affrick hold.
For me, in sooth, no Muse but one I know,
    Phrases and problems from my reach do grow;
And strange things cost too deare for my poor sprites.
    How then? euen thus: in Stellaes face I reed
        What Love and Beautie be; then all my deed
        But copying is, what in her Nature writes.

IV

Vertue, alas, now let me take some rest;
  Thou setst a bate betweene my will and wit;
If vaine Love haue my simple soule opprest,
  Leaue what thou lik'st not, deale thou not with it.
Thy scepter vse in some old Catoes brest,
  Churches or Schooles are for thy seat more fit;
I do confesse (pardon a fault confest)
  My mouth too tender is for thy hard bit.
But if that needes thou wilt vsurping be
  The little reason that is left in me,
And still th'effect of thy perswasions prooue,
  I sweare, my heart such one shall show to thee,
    That shrines in flesh so true a deitie,
    That, Virtue, thou thyself shalt be in love.

V

It is most true that eyes are form'd to serue
  The inward light, and that the heauenly part
Ought to be King, from whose rules who do swerue,
  Rebels to nature, striue for their owne smart.
It is most true, what we call Cupids dart
  An image is, which for ourselues we carue,
And, foolse, adore in temple of our hart,
  Till that good god make church and churchmen starue.
True, that true beautie virtue is indeed,
  Whereof this beautie can be but a shade,
Which, elements with mortal mixture breed.
  True, that on earth we are but pilgrims made,
    And should in soule up to our countrey moue:
    True, and yet true that I must Stella love.

VI

Some lovers speake, when they their Muses entertaine,
  Of hopes begot by feare, of wot not what desires,
Of force of heau'nly beames infusing hellish paine,
  Of liuing deaths, dere wounds, faire storms, and freesing
                                   fires:
Some one his song in Ioue and Ioues strange tales attires,
  Bordred with buls and swans, powdred with golden
                                   raine:
Another, humbler wit, to shepherds pipe retires,
  Yet hiding royall bloud full oft in rurall vaine.
To some a sweetest plaint a sweetest stile affords:
  While teares poure out his inke, and sighes breathe out
                              his words,
His paper pale despaire, and pain his pen doth moue.
  I can speake what I feele, and feele as much as they,
    But thinke that all the map of my state I display
    When trembling voyce brings forth, that I do Stella love.

VII

When Nature made her chief worke, Stellas eyes,
　　In colour blacke why wrapt she beames so bright?
Would she in beamy blacke, like Painter wise,
　　Frame daintiest lustre, mixt of shades and light?
Or did she else that sober hue deuise,
　　In obiect best to knitt and strength our sight;
Least, if no vaile these braue gleames did disguise,
　　They, sunlike, should more dazle then delight?
Or would she her miraculous power show,
　　That, whereas blacke seems Beauties contrary,
She euen in black doth make all beauties flow?
　　Both so, and thus, she, minding Love should be
　　　　Plac'd euer there, gaue him this mourning weede
　　　　To honour all their deaths who for her bleed.

VIII

Love, borne in Greece, of late fled from his natiue place,
  Forc't, by a tedious proof, that Turkish hardned heart
Is not fit mark to pierce with his fine-pointed dart,
  And pleas'd with our soft peace, staide here his flying
                                        race:
But, finding these north clymes too coldly him embrace,
  Not vsde to frozen clips, he straue to find some part
Where with most ease and warmth he might employ his
                                        art;
  At length he perch'd himself in Stellaes ioyful face,
Whose faire skin, beamy eyes, like morning sun on snow,
  Deceiu'd the quaking boy, who thought, from so pure
                                        light,
Effects of liuely heat must needs in nature grow:
  But she, most faire, most cold, made him thence take his
                                        flight
    To my close heart, where, while some firebrands he did
                                        lay,
    He burnt un'wares his wings, and cannot flie away.

IX

Queen Virtues Court, which some call Stellaes face,
   Prepar'd by Natures choicest furniture,
Hath his front built of alabaster pure;
   Gold is the couering of that stately place.
The door, by which sometimes comes forth her grace,
   Red porphir is, which locke of pearl makes sure,
Whose porches rich (which name of chekes indure)
   Marble, mixt red and white, doe interlace.
The windowes now, through which this heau'nly guest
   Looks ouer the world, and can find nothing such,
Which dare claime from those lights the name of best,
   Of touch they are, that without touch do touch,
     Which Cupids self, from Beauties mine did draw:
     Of touch they are, and poore I am their straw.

X

Reason, in faith thou art well seru'd that still
    Wouldst brabbling be with Sense and Love in me;
I rather wisht thee clime the Muses hill;
    Or reach the fruite of Natures choycest tree;
Or seek heau'ns course or heau'ns inside to see:
    Why shouldst thou toil our thorny soile to till?
Leaue Sense, and those which Senses obiects be;
    Deale thou with powers of thoughts, leaue Love to Will.
But thou wouldst needs fight with both Love and Sence,
    With sword of wit giuing wounds of dispraise,
Till downe-right blowes did foyle thy cunning fence;
    For, soone as they strake thee with Stellas rayes,
        Reason, thou kneeld'st, and offred'st straight to proue,
        By reason good, good reason her to love.

XI

In truth, O Love, with what a boyish kind
   Thou doest proceed in thy most serious ways,
That when the heau'n to thee his best displayes,
   Yet of that best thou leau'st the best behinde!
For, like a childe that some faire booke doth find,
   With gilded leaues or colour'd vellum playes,
Or, at the most, on some fine picture stayes,
   But neuer heeds the fruit of Writers mind;
So when thou saw'st, in Natures cabinet,
   Stella, thou straight lookst babies in her eyes:
In her chekes pit thou didst thy pitfold set,
   And in her breast bo-peepe or crouching lies,
     Playing and shining in each outward part;
     But, fool, seekst not to get into her heart.

XII

Cupid, because thou shin'st in Stellaes eyes
   That from her locks thy day-nets none scapes free
That those lips sweld so full of thee they be
   That her sweet breath makes oft thy flames to rise
That in her breast thy pap well sugred lies
   That her grace gracious makes thy wrongsthat she,
What words soere shee speake, perswades for thee
   That her clere voice lifts thy fame to the skies,
Thou countest Stella thine, like those whose powers
   Hauing got vp a breach by fighting well,
Crie Victorie, this faire day all is ours!
   O no; her heart is such a cittadell,
      So fortified with wit, stor'd with disdaine,
      That to win it is all the skill and paine.

XIII

Phoebus was iudge betweene Ioue, Mars, and Love,
  Of those three gods, whose armes the fairest were.
Ioues golden shield did sable eagles beare,
  Whose talons held young Ganimed aboue:
But in vert field Mars bare a golden speare,
  Which through a bleeding heart his point did shoue:
Each had his creast; Mars carried Venus glove,
  Ioue on his helmet the thunderbolt did reare.
Cupid then smiles, for on his crest there lies
  Stellas faire haire; her face he makes his shield,
Where roses gules are borne in siluer field.
  Phoebus drew wide the curtaines of the skies,
    To blaze these last, and sware deuoutly then,
    The first, thus matcht, were scantly gentlemen.

XIV

Alas, haue I not pain enough, my friend,
  Upon whose breast a fiecer Gripe doth tire
Than did on him who first stale down the fire,
  While Love on me doth all his quiuer spend,
But with your rhubarbe words ye must contend
  To grieue me worse, in saying that Desire
Doth plunge my wel-form'd soul euen in the mire
  Of sinfull thoughts, which do in ruin end?
If that be sinne which doth the manners frame,
  Well staid with truth in word and faith of deede,
Ready of wit, and fearing nought but shame;
  If that be sin which in fixt hearts doth breed
    A loathing of all loose unchastitie,
    Then love is sin, and let me sinfull be.

XV

You that do search for euery purling spring
  Which from the ribs of old Parnassus flowes,
And euery flower, not sweet perhaps, which growes
  Neere thereabouts, into your poesie wring;
Ye that do dictionaries methode bring
  Into your rimes, running in rattling rowes;
You that poore Petrarchs long deceased woes
  With new-borne sighes and denisen'd wit do sing;
You take wrong wayes; those far-fet helps be such
  As do bewray a want of inward tuch,
And sure, at length stol'n goods doe come to light:
  But if, both for your love and skill, your name
    You seek to nurse at fullest breasts of Fame,
    Stella behold, and then begin to indite.

XVI

In nature, apt to like, when I did see
  Beauties which were of many carrets fine,
My boiling sprites did thither then incline,
  And, Love, I thought that I was full of thee:
But finding not those restlesse flames in mee,
  Which others said did make their souls to pine,
I thought those babes of some pinnes hurt did whine,
  By my soul iudging what Loves paine might be.
But while I thus with this young lion plaid,
  Mine eyes (shall I say curst or blest?) beheld
Stella: now she is nam'd, neede more be said?
  In her sight I a lesson new haue speld.
    I now haue learnd love right, and learnd euen so
    As they that being poysond poyson know.

XVII

His mother deere, Cupid offended late,
   Because that Mars, growne slacker in her love,
With pricking shot he did not throughly moue
   To keepe the place of their first loving state.
The boy refusde for fear of Marses hate,
   Who threatned stripes if he his wrath did proue;
But she, in chafe, him from her lap did shoue,
   Brake bowe, brake shafts, while Cupid weeping sate;
Till that his grandame Nature, pitying it,
   Of Stellaes brows made him two better bowes,
And in her eyes of arrows infinit.
   O how for ioy he leaps! O how he crowes!
     And straight therewith, like wags new got to play,
     Falls to shrewd turnes! And I was in his way.

XVIII

With what sharp checkes I in myself am shent
  When into Reasons audite I do goe,
And by iust counts my selfe a bankrout know
  Of all those goods which heauen to me hath lent;
Unable quite to pay euen Natures rent,
  Which unto it by birthright I do ow;
And, which is worse, no good excuse can showe,
  But that my wealth I haue most idly spent!
My youth doth waste, my knowledge brings forth toyes,
  My wit doth striue those passions to defende,
Which, for reward, spoil it with vain annoyes.
  I see, my course to lose myself doth bend;
    I see: and yet no greater sorrow take
    Than that I lose no more for Stellas sake.

XIX

On Cupids bowe how are my heart-strings bent,
   That see my wracke, and yet embrace the same!
When most I glory, then I feele most shame;
   I willing run, yet while I run repent;
My best wits still their own disgrace inuent:
   My very inke turns straight to Stellas name;
And yet my words, as them my pen doth frame,
   Auise them selues that they are vainely spent:
For though she passe all things, yet what is all
   That unto me, who fare like him that both
Lookes to the skies and in a ditch doth fall?
   O let me prop my mind, yet in his growth,
     And not in nature for best fruits unfit.
     Scholler, saith Love, bend hitherward your wit.

XX

Fly, fly, my friends; I haue my deaths wound, fly;
  See there that Boy, that murthring Boy I say,
Who like a theefe hid in dark bush doth ly,
  Till bloudy bullet get him wrongfull pray.
So, tyran he no fitter place could spie,
  Nor so faire leuell in so secret stay,
As that sweet black which veils the heau'nly eye;
  There with his shot himself he close doth lay.
Poore passenger, pass now thereby I did,
  And staid, pleas'd with the prospect of the place,
While that black hue from me the the bad guest hid:
  But straight I saw the motions of lightning grace,
    And then descried the glistrings of his dart:
    But ere I could flie thence, it pierc'd my heart.

XXI

Your words, my friend, (right healthfull caustiks), blame
  My young mind marde, whom Love doth windlas so;
That mine owne writings, like bad seruants, show
  My wits quicke in vaine thoughts, in vertue lame;
That Plato I read for nought but if he tame
  Such coltish yeeres; that to my birth I owe
Nobler desires, lest else that friendly foe,
  Great expectation, wear a train of shame:
For since mad March great promise made of mee,
  If now the May of my yeeres much decline,
What can be hop'd my haruest-time will be?
  Sure, you say well, Your wisedomes golden myne
    Dig deepe with Learnings spade. Now tell me this:
    Hath this world aught so fair as Stella is?

XXII

In highest way of heau'n the Sun did ride,
  Progressing then from fair Twinnes golden place,
Hauing no mask of clouds before his face,
  But streaming forth of heate in his chiefe pride;
When some fair ladies, by hard promise tied,
  On horsebacke met him in his furious race;
Yet each prepar'd with fannes wel-shading grace
  From that foes wounds their tender skinnes to hide.
Stella alone with face unarmed marcht,
  Either to do like him which open shone,
Or carelesse of the wealth, because her owne.
  Yet were the hid and meaner beauties parcht;
    Her dainties bare went free: the cause was this:
    The sun, that others burn'd, did her but kisse.

XXIII

The curious wits, seeing dull pensiuenesse
   Bewray it self in my long-settl'd eies
Whence those same fumes of melancholy rise,
   With idle paines and missing ayme do guesse.
Some, that know how my spring I did addresse,
   Deem that my Muse some fruit of knowledge plies;
Others, because the prince my seruice tries,
   Thinke that I think State errours to redress:
But harder iudges iudge ambitions rage:
   Scourge of itselfe, still climbing slipperie place:
Holds my young brain captiu'd in golden cage.
   O fooles, or ouer-wise. alas, the race
      Of all my thoughts hath neither stop nor start
      But only Stellaes eyes and Stellaes heart.

XXIV

Rich fooles there be whose base and filthy heart
  Lies hatching still the goods wherein they flow,
And damning their own selues to Tantals smart,
  Wealth breeding want; more rich, more wretched growe:
Yet to those fooles Heau'n doth such wit impart
  As what their hands do hold, their heads do know,
And knowing love, and loving lay apart
  As sacred things, far from all dangers show.
But that rich foole, who by blind Fortunes lot
  The richest gemme of love and life enioys,
And can with foule abuse such beauties blot;
  Let him, depriu'd of sweet but unfelt ioys,
    Exild for ay from those high treasures which
    He knowes not, grow in only folly rich!

XXV

The wisest scholler of the wight most wise
   By Phoebus doom, with sugred sentence sayes,
That vertue, if it once met with our eyes,
   Strange flames of love it in our souls would raise;
But for that man with paine this truth descries,
   Whiles he each thing in Senses balance wayes,
And so nor will nor can behold those skies
   Which inward sunne to heroick mind displaies
Vertue of late, with vertuous care to ster
   Love of herself, tooke Stellas shape, that she
To mortall eyes might sweetly shine in her.
   It is most true; for since I her did see,
      Vertues great beauty in that face I proue,
      And find th' effect, for I do burn in love.

XXVI

Though dustie wits dare scorne Astrologie,
   And fooles can thinke those lampes of purest light
Whose numbers, waies, greatnesse, eternity,
   Promising wonders, wonder do inuite
To haue for no cause birthright in the sky
   But for to spangle the black weeds of Night;
Or for some brawl which in that chamber hie,
   They should still dance to please a gazers sight.
For me, I do Nature unidle know,
   And know great causes great effects procure;
And know those bodies high raigne on the low.
   And if these rules did fail, proof makes me sure,
      Who oft fore-see my after-following race,
      By only those two starres in Stellaes face.

XXVII

Because I oft in darke abstracted guise
  Seeme most alone in greatest company,
With dearth of words, or answers quite awrie,
  To them that would make speech of speech arise;
They deeme, and of their doome the runour flies,
  That poison foul of bubbling pride doth lie
So in my swelling breast, that only I
  Fawne on my selfe, and others do despise.
Yet pride I thinke doth not my soule possesse
  (Which looks too oft in his unflatt'ring glasse):
But one worse fault, ambition, I confesse,
  That makes me oft my best friends ouerpasse,
    Unseene, unheard, while thought to highest place
    Bends all his powers, euen unto Stellaes grace.

XXVIII

You that with Allegories curious frame
  Of others children changelings vse to make,
With me those pains, for Gods sake, do not take:
  I list not dig so deep for brazen fame,
When I say Stella I do meane the same
  Princesse of beauty for whose only sake
The raines of Love I love, though neuer slake,
  And ioy therein, though nations count it shame.
I beg no subiect to vse eloquence,
  Nor in hid wayes to guide philosophy:
Looke at my hands for no such quintessence;
  But know that I in pure simplicitie
    Breathe out the flames which burn within my heart,
    Love onely reading unto me this arte.

XXIX

Like some weak lords neighbord by mighty kings,
  To keep themselues and their chief cities free,
Do easily yeeld that all their coasts may be
  Ready to store their campes of needfull things;
So Stellas heart, finding what power Love brings
  To keep it selfe in life and liberty,
Doth willing graunt that in the frontiers he
  Vse all to helpe his other conquerings.
And thus her heart escapes; but thus her eyes
  Serue him with shot, her lips his heralds are,
Her breasts his tents, legs his triumphall car,
  Her flesh his food, her skin his armour braue.
    And I, but for because my prospect lies
    Upon that coast, am given vp for slaue.

XXX

Whether the Turkish new moone minded be
  To fill her hornes this yeere on Christian coast;
How Poles right king means without leaue of host
  To warm with ill-made fire cold Muscouy;
If French can yet three parts in one agree:
  What now the Dutch in their full diets boast;
How Holland hearts, now so good townes be lost,
  Trust in the shade of pleasant Orange-tree;
How Vlster likes of that same golden bit
  Wherewith my father once made it half tame;
If in the Scotch Court be no weltring yet;
  These questions busy wits to me do frame:
    I, cumbred with good manners, answer doe,
    But know not how; for still I thinke of you.

XXXI

With how sad steps, O Moone, thou climbst the skies!
   How silently, and with how wanne a face!
What, may it be that euen in heau'nly place
   That busie archer his sharpe arrowes tries?
Sure, if that long-with-love-acquainted eyes
   Can iudge of love, thou feel'st a lovers case,
I reade it in thy lookes: thy languist grace,
   To me that feele the like, thy state discries.
Then, eu'n of fellowship, O Moone, tell me,
   Is constant love deem'd there but want of wit?
Are beauties there as proud as here they be?
   Do they aboue love to be lov'd, and yet
      Those lovers scorn whom that love doth possesse?
      Do they call vertue there ungratefulnesse?

XXXII

Morpheus, the liuely sonne of deadly Sleepe,
  Witnesse of life to them that liuing die,
A prophet oft, and oft an historie,
  A poet eke, as humours fly or creepe;
Since thou in me so sure a power dost keepe,
  That neuer I with clos'd-vp sense do lie,
But by thy worke my Stella I descrie,
  Teaching blind eyes both how to smile and weepe;
Vouchsafe, of all acquaintance, this to tell,
  Whence hast thou ivory, rubies, pearl, and gold,
To shew her skin, lips, teeth, and head so well?
  Foole! answers he; no Indes such treasures hold;
    But from thy heart, while my sire charmeth thee,
    Sweet Stellas image I do steal to mee.

XXXIII

I might (unhappy word!) O me, I might,
  And then I would not, or could not, see my blisse,
Till now wrapt in a most infernall night,
  I find how heau'nly day, wretch! I did misse.
Hart, rend thyself, thou dost thyself but right;
  No lovely Paris made thy Hellen his;
No force, no fraud robd thee of thy delight,
  Nor Fortune of thy fortune author is,
But to my selfe my selfe did giue the blow,
  While too much wit, forsooth, so troubled me
That I respects for both our sakes must show:
  And yet could not, by rysing morne fore-see
    How fair a day was near: O punisht eyes,
    That I had bene more foolish, or more wise!

XXXIV

Come, let me write. And to what end? To ease
  A burthen'd heart. How can words ease, which are
The glasses of thy dayly-vexing care?
  Oft cruel fights well pictur'd-forth do please.
Art not asham'd to publish thy disease?
  Nay, that may breed my fame, it is so rare.
But will not wise men thinke thy words fond ware?
  Then be they close, and so none shall displease.
What idler thing then speake and not be hard?
  What harder thing then smart and not to speake?
Peace, foolish wit! with wit my wit is mard.
  Thus write I, while I doubt to write, and wreake
    My harmes in inks poor losse. Perhaps some find
    Stellas great powers, that so confuse my mind.

XXXV

What may words say, or what may words not say,
   Where Truth itself must speake like Flatterie?
Within what bounds can one his liking stay,
   Where Nature doth with infinite agree?
What Nestors counsell can my flames alay,
   Since Reasons self doth blow the coale in me?
And, ah, what hope that Hope should once see day,
   Where Cupid is sworn page to Chastity?
Honour is honour'd that thou dost possesse
   Him as thy slaue, and now long-needy Fame
Doth euen grow rich, meaning my Stellaes name.
   Wit learnes in thee perfection to expresse:
     Not thou by praise, but praise in thee is raisde:
     It is a praise to praise, when thou art praisde.

XXXVI

Stella, whence doth these new assaults arise,
  A conquerd yeelding ransackt heart to winne,
Whereto long since, through my long-battred eyes,
  Whole armies of thy beauties entred in?
And there, long since, Love, thy lieutenant, lies;
  My forces razde, thy banners raisd within:
Of conquest, do not these effects suffice,
  But wilt new warre upon thine own begin?
With so sweet voice, and by sweet Nature so
  In sweetest strength, so sweetly skild withall,
In sweetest stratagems sweete Art can show,
  That not my soul, which at thy foot did fall
    Long since, forc'd by thy beams, but stone nor tree,
    By Sences priviledge, can scape from thee!

XXXVII

My mouth doth water, and my breast doth swell,
  My tongue doth itch, my thoughts in labour be:
Listen then, lordings, with good ear to me,
  For of my life I must a riddle tell.
Toward Auroras Court a nymph doth dwell,
  Rich in all beauties which mans eye can see;
Beauties so farre from reach of words that we
  Abase her praise saying she doth excell;
Rich in the treasure of deseru'd renowne,
  Rich in the riches of a royall heart,
Rich in those gifts which giue th'eternall crowne;
  Who, though most rich in these and eu'ry part
    Which make the patents of true worldy blisse,
    Hath no misfortune but that Rich she is.

XXXVIII

This night, while sleepe begins with heauy wings
  To hatch mine eyes, and that unbitted thought
Doth fall to stray, and my chief powres are brought
  To leaue the scepter of all subiect things;
The first that straight my fancys errour brings
  Unto my mind is Stellas image, wrought
By Loves own selfe, but with so curious drought
  That she, methinks, not onley shines but sings.
I start, look, hearke: but in what closde-vp sence
  Was held, in opend sense it flies away,
Leauing me nought but wayling eloquence.
  I, seeing better sights in sights decay,
    Cald it anew, and wooed Sleepe again;
    But him, her host, that unkind guest had slain.

XXXIX

Come, Sleepe! O Sleepe, the certaine knot of peace,
  The baiting-place of wit, the balme of woe,
The poor mans wealth, the prisoners release,
  Th' indifferent iudge betweene the high and low!
With shield of proofe shield me from out the prease
  Of those fierce darts Despaire at me doth throw.
O make in me those ciuil wars to cease;
  I will good tribute pay, if thou do so.
Take thou of me smooth pillowes, sweetest bed,
  A chamber deafe of noise and blind of light,
A rosie garland and a weary hed:
  And if these things, as being thine in right,
    Moue not thy heauy grace, thou shalt in me,
    Liuelier then else-where, Stellaes image see.

XL

As good to write, as for to lie and grone.
  O Stella deare, how much thy powre hath wrought,
That hast my mind (now of the basest) brought
  My still-kept course, while others sleepe, to mone!
Alas, if from the height of Vertues throne
  Thou canst vouchsafe the influence of a thought
Upon a wretch that long thy grace hath sought,
  Weigh then how I by thee am ouerthrowne,
And then thinke thus: although thy beautie be
  Made manifest by such a victorie,
Yet noble conquerours do wreckes auoid.
  Since then thou hast so farre subdued me
    That in my heart I offer still to thee,
    O do not let thy temple be destroyd!

XLI

Hauing this day my horse, my hand, my launce
   Guided so well that I obtain'd the prize,
Both by the iudgement of the English eyes
   And of some sent from that sweet enemy Fraunce;
Horsemen my skill in horsemanship aduaunce,
   Towne folkes my strength; a daintier iudge applies
His praise to sleight which from good vse doth rise;
   Some luckie wits impute it but to chance;
Others, because of both sides I doe take
   My blood from them who did excell in this,
Thinke Nature me a man-at-armes did make.
   How farre they shot awrie! The true cause is,
     Stella lookt on, and from her heau'nly face
     Sent forth the beames which made so faire my race.

XLII

O eyes, which do the spheres of beauty moue;
　Whose beames be ioyes, whose ioyes all vertues be,
Who, while they make Love conquer, conquer Love;
　The schooles where Venus hath learnd chastitie:
O eyes, where humble lookes most glorious proue,
　Onely lov'd Tyrans, iust in cruelty,
Do not, O doe not, from poore me remoue:
　Keep still my zenith, euer shine on me;
For though I neuer see them, but straightwayes
　My life forgets to nourish languisht sprites,
Yet still on me, O eyes, dart down your rayes!
　And if from majestie of sacred lights
　　Oppressing mortal sense my death proceed,
　　Wraceks triumphs be which Love hie set doth breed.

XLIII

Faire eyes, sweet lips, dear heart, that foolish I
   Could hope, by Cupids help, on you to pray,
Since to himselfe he doth your gifts apply,
   As his maine force, choise sport, and easefull stay!
For when he will see who dare him gain-say,
   Then with those eyes he looeks: lo, by and by
Each soule doth at Loves feet his weapons lay,
   Glad if for her he giue them leaue to die.
When he will play, then in her lips he is,
   Where, blushing red, that Loves selfe them doe love,
With either lip he doth the other kisse;
   But when he will, for quiets sake, remoue
     From all the world, her heart is then his rome,
     Where well he knowes no man to him can come.

XLIV

My words I know do well set forth my minde;
   My mind bemones his sense of inward smart;
Such smart may pitie claim of any hart;
   Her heart, sweet heart, is of no tygres kind:
And yet she heares and yet no pitie I find,
   But more I cry, less grace she doth impart.
Alas, what cause is there so ouerthwart
   That Nobleness it selfe makes thus unkind?
I much do ghesse, yet finde no truth saue this,
   That when the breath of my complaints doth tuch
Those dainty doors unto the Court of Blisse,
   The heau'nly nature of that place is such,
      That, once come there, the sobs of mine annoyes
      Are metamorphos'd straight to tunes of ioyes.

XLV

Stella oft sees the very face of wo
  Painted in my beclowded stormie face,
But cannot skill to pitie my disgrace,
  Not though thereof the cause herself she know:
Yet, hearing late a fable which did show
  Of lovers neuer knowne, a grieuous case,
Pitie thereof gate in her breast such place,
  That, from that sea deriu'd, teares spring did flow.
Alas, if Fancie, drawne by imag'd things
  Though false, yet with free scope, more grace doth breed
Than seruants wracke, where new doubts honour brings;
  Then thinke, my deare, that you in me do reed
    Of lovers ruine some thrise-sad tragedie.
    I am not I: pitie the tale of me.

XLVI

I curst thee oft, I pitie now thy case,
  Blind-hitting Boy, since she that thee and me
Rules with a becke, so tyranniseth thee,
  That thou must want or food or dwelling-place,
For she protests to banish thee her face.
  Her face! O Love, a roge thou then shouldst be,
If Love learne not alone to love and see,
  Without desire to feed of further grace.
Alas, poor wag, that now a scholler art
  To such a schoolmistresse, whose lessons new
Thou needs must misse, and so thou needs must smart.
  Yet, deare, let me his pardon get of you,
    So long, though he from book myche to desire,
    Till without fewell you can make hot fire.

XLVII

What, haue I thus betray'd my libertie?
  Can those blacke beames such burning markes engraue
In my free side, or am I borne a slaue,
  Whose necke becomes such yoke of tyrannie?
Or want I sense to feel my misery,
  Or sprite, disdaine of such disdaine to haue,
Who for long faith, tho' daily helpe I craue,
  May get no almes, but scorne of beggarie.
Vertue, awake! Beautie but beautie is;
  I may, I must, I can, I will, I do
Leaue following that which it is gain to misse.
   Let her goe! Soft, but here she comes! Goe to,
    Unkind, I love you not! O me, that eye
    Doth make my heart to giue my tongue the lie!

XLVIII

Soules ioy, bend not those morning starres from me
  Where Vertue is made strong by Beauties might;
Where Love is chasteness, Paine doth learn delight,
  And Humbleness growes one with Maiesty.
Whateuer may ensue, O let me be
  Copartner of the riches of that sight.
Let not mine eyes be hel-driu'n from that light;
  O look, O shine, O let me die, and see.
For though I oft myself of them bemone
  That through my heart their beamie darts be gone,
Whose cureless wounds euen now most freshly bleed,
  Yet since my death-wound is already got,
    Deere killer, spare not thy sweete-cruell shot:
    A kinde of grace it is to slaye with speed.

XLIX

I on my horse, and Love on me, doth trie
  Our horsemanships, while by strange worke I proue
A horsman to my horse, a horse to Love,
  And now mans wrongs in me, poor beast! descrie.
The raines wherewith my rider doth me tie
  Are humbled thoughts, which bit of reuerence moue,
Curb'd-in with feare, but with gilt bosse aboue
  Of hope, which makes it seem fair to the eye:
The wand is will; thou, Fancie, saddle art,
  Girt fast by Memorie; and while I spurre
My horse, he spurres with sharpe desire my hart.
  He sits me fast, howeuer I do sturre,
    And now hath made me to his hand so right,
    That in the manage my selfe take delight.

L

Stella, the fullnesse of my thoughts of thee
  Cannot be staid within my panting breast,
But they do swell and struggle forth of me,
  Till that in words thy figure be exprest:
And yet, as soone as they so formed be,
  According to my lord Loves oene behest,
With sad eies I their weak proportion see
  To portrait that which in this world is best.
So that I cannot chuse but write my mind,
  And cannot chuse but put out what I write,
While these poor babes their death in birth do find;
  And now my pen these lines had dashed quite
    But that they stopt his fury from the same,
    Because their forefront bare sweet Stellas name.

LI

Pardon mine ears, both I and they do pray,
　So may your tongue still flauntingly proceed
To them that do such entertainment need,
　So may you still haue somewhat new to say.
On silly me do not the burthen lay
　Of all the graue conceits your braine doth breed,
But find some Hercules to beare, insteed
　Of Atlas tyrd, your wisedoms heau'nly sway.
For me, while you discourse of courtly tides,
　Of cunningest fishers in most troubled streames,
Of straying waies, when valiant Errour guides,
　Meanewhile my heart confers with Stellas beames,
　　And is e'en woe that so sweet comedie
　　By such unsuted speech should hindred be.

LII

A strife is growne between Vertue and Love,
  While each pretends that Stella must be his:
Her eyes, her lips, her all, saith Love, do this,
  Since they do weare his badge, most firmly proue.
But Virtue thus that title doth disproue,
  That Stella (O dear name!) that Stella is
That vertuous soule, sure heire of heau'nly blisse.
  Not this faire outside, which our heart doth moue.
And therefore, though her beautie and her grace
  Be Loves indeed, in Stellas selfe he may
By no pretence claime any manner place.
  Well, Love, since this demurre our sute doth stay,
    Let Vertue haue that Stellaes selfe, yet thus,
    That Vertue but that body graunt to vs.

LIII

In martiall sports I had my cunning tride,
   And yet to breake more staues did mee addresse,
While, with the peoples shouts, I must confesse,
   Youth, lucke, and praise euen fil'd my veines with pride;
When Cupid, hauing me, his slaue, descride
   In Marses livery prauncing in the presse,
What now, Sir Foole! said he, (I would no lesse:)
   Looke here, I say! I look'd, and Stella spide,
Who, hard by, made a window send forth light.
   My heart then quak'd, then dazled were mine eyes,
One hand forgat to rule, th'other to fight,
   Nor trumpets sound I heard, nor friendly cries:
     My foe came on, and beate the air for me,
     Till that her blush taught me my shame to see.

LIV

Because I breathe not love to euery one,
   Nor doe not vse sette colours for to weare,
Nor nourish speciall locks of vowed haire,
   Nor giue each speech a full point of a grone,
The Courtly Nymphes, acquainted with the mone
   Of them wich in their lips Loves Standard beare:
What, he! (say they of me): now I dare sweare
   He cannot love; no,no, let him alone.
And thinke so still, so Stella know my minde;
   Profess in deede I do not Cupids art;
But you, fair maides, at length this true shall find,
   That his right badge is but worne in the hart:
     Dumbe Swans, not chattering Pyes, do lovers proue;
     They love indeed who quake to say they love.

LV

Muses, I oft inuoked your holy ayde,
  With choisest flowers my speech t' engarland so,
That it, despisde, in true but naked shew
  Might winne some grace in your sweet grace arraid;
And oft whole troupes of saddest words I staid,
  Striuing abroad a-foraging to go,
Untill by your inspiring I might know
  How their blacke banner might be best displaid.
But now I meane no more your helpe to try,
  Nor other sugring of my speech to proue,
But on her name incessantly to cry;
  For let me but name her whom I doe love,
    So sweet sounds straight mine eare and heart do hit,
    That I well finde no eloquence like it.

LVI

Fy, schoole of Patience, fy! your Lesson is
    Far, far too long to learne it without booke:
What, a whole weeke without one peece of looke,
    And thinke I should not your large precepts misse!
When I might reade those Letters faire of blisse
    Which in her face teach vertue, I could brooke
Somwhat thy leaden counsels, which I tooke
    As of a friend that meant not much amisse.
But now that I, alas, doe want her sight,
    What, dost thou thinke that I can euer take
In thy cold stuffe a flegmatike delight?
    No, Patience; if thou wilt my good, then make
        Her come and heare with patience my desire,
        And then with patience bid me beare my fire.

LVII

Who hauing made, with many fights, his owne
   Each sence of mine, each gift, each power of mind;
Growne now his slaues, he forst them out to find
   The thorowest words fit for Woes selfe to grone,
Hoping that when they might finde Stella alone,
   Before she could prepare to be unkind,
Her soule, arm'd but with such a dainty rind,
   Should soone be pierc'd with sharpnesse of the mone.
She heard my plaints, and did not onely heare,
   But them, so sweet is she, most sweetly sing,
With that faire breast making Woes darknesse cleare.
   A pretie case; I hoped her to bring
      To feele my griefe; and she, with face and voyce,
      So sweets my paines that my paines me reioyce.

LVIII

Doubt there hath beene when with his golden chaine
  The orator so farre mens hearts doth bind,
That no pace else their guided steps can find
  But as he them more short or slack doth raine;
Whether with words this soueraignty he gaine,
  Cloth'd with fine tropes, with strongest reasons lin'd,
Or else pronouncing grace, wherewith his mind
  Prints his owne liuely forme in rudest braine.
Now iudge by this: in piercing phrases late
  Th' Anatomie of all my woes I wrate;
Stellas sweet breath the same to me did reed.
  O voyce, O face! maugre my speeches might,
    Which wooed wo, most rauishing delight
    Euen those sad words euen in sad me did breed.

.

LIX

Deere, why make you more of a dog then me?
   If he doe love, I burne, I burne in love;
If he waite well, I neuer thence would moue;
   If he be faire, yet but a dog can be;
Little he is, so little worth is he;
   He barks, my songs thine owne voyce oft doth proue;
Bidden, perhaps he fetched thee a glove,
   But I, unbid, fetch euen my soule to thee.
Yet, while I languish, him that bosome clips,
   That lap doth lap, nay lets, in spite of spite,
This sowre-breath'd mate taste of those sugred lips.
   Alas, if you graunt onely such delight
     To witlesse things, then Love, I hope (since wit
     Becomes a clog) will soone ease me of it.

.

LX

When my good Angell guides me to the place
　　Where all my good I doe in Stella see,
That heau'n of ioyes throwes onely downe on me
　　Thundring disdaines and lightnings of disgrace;
But when the ruggedst step of Fortunes race
　　Makes me fall from her sight, then sweetly she,
With words wherein the Muses treasures be,
　　Shewes love and pitie to my absent case.
Now I, wit-beaten long by hardest fate,
　　So dull am, that I cannot looke into
The ground of this fierce love and lovely hate.
　　Then, some good body, tell me how I do,
　　　Whose presence absence, absence presence is;
　　　Blest in my curse, and cursed in my blisse.

LXI

Oft with true sighs, oft with uncalled teares,
   Now with slow words, now with dumbe eloquence,
I Stellas eyes assaid, inuade her eares;
   But this, at last, is her sweet breath'd defence:
That who indeed in-felt affection beares,
   So captiues to his Saint both soule and sence,
That, wholly hers, all selfenesse he forbeares,
   Then his desires he learnes, his liues course thence.
Now, since her chast mind hates this love in me,
   With chastned mind I straight must shew that she
Shall quickly me from what she hates remoue.
   O Doctor Cupid, thou for me reply;
     Driu'n else to graunt, by Angels Sophistrie,
     That I love not without I leaue to love.

LXII

Late tyr'd with wo, euen ready for to pine
   With rage of love, I cald my Love unkind;
She in whose eyes love, though unfelt, doth shine,
   Sweet said, that I true love in her should find.
I ioyed; but straight thus watred was my wine;
   That love she did, but lov'd a love not blind;
Which would not let me, whom shee lov'd, decline
   From nobler course, fit for my birth and mind:
And therefore, by her loves Authority,
   Wild me these tempests of vaine love to flie,
And anchor fast my selfe on Vertues shore.
   Alas, if this the only mettall be
     Of love new-coin'd to help my beggary,
     Deere, love me not, that you may love me more.

LXIII

O grammer-rules, O now your vertues show;
  So children still reade you with awfull eyes,
As my young doue may, in your precepts wise,
  Her graunt to me by her owne vertue know:
For late, with heart most hie, with eyes most lowe,
  I crau'd the thing which euer she denies;
Shee, lightning love, displaying Venus skies,
  Least once should not be heard, twise said, No, no.
Sing then, my Muse, now Io Pæn sing;
  Heau'ns enuy not at my high triumphing,
But grammers force with sweete successe confirme:
  For grammer says, (O this, deare Stella, say,)
    For grammer sayes, (to grammer who sayes nay?)
    That in one speech two negatiues affirme!

First Song

Doubt you to whom my Muse these notes entendeth,
Which now my breast, surcharg'd, to musick lendeth!
To you, to you, all song of praise is due,
Only in you my song begins and endeth.

Who hath the eyes which marrie state with pleasure!
Who keeps the key of Natures cheifest treasure!
To you, to you, all song of praise is due,
Only for you the heau'n forgate all measure.

Who hath the lips, where wit in fairnesse raigneth!
Who womankind at once both deckes and stayneth!
To you, to you, all song of praise is due,
Onely by you Cupid his crowne maintaineth.

Who hath the feet, whose step all sweetnesse planteth!
Who else, for whom Fame worthy trumpets wanteth!
To you, to you, all song of praise is due,
Onely to you her scepter Venus granteth.

Who hath the breast, whose milk doth patience nourish!
Whose grace is such, that when it chides doth cherish!
To you, to you, all song of praise is due,
Onelie through you the tree of life doth flourish.

Who hath the hand which, without stroke, subdueth!
Who long-dead beautie with increase reneueth!
To you, to you, all song of praise is due,
Onely at you all enuie hopelesse rueth.

Who hath the haire, which, loosest, fastest tieth!
Who makes a man liue, then glad when he dieth!
To you, to you, all song of praise is due,
Only of you the flatterer neuer lieth.

Who hath the voyce, which soule from sences thunders!
Whose force, but yours, the bolts of beautie thunders!
To you, to you, all song of praise is due,
Only with you not miracles are wonders.

Doubt you, to whome my Muse these notes intendeth,
Which now my breast, oercharg'd, to musicke lendeth!
To you, to you, all song of praise is due:
Only in you my song begins and endeth.

LXIV

No more, my deare, no more these counsels trie;
  O giue my passions leaue to run their race;
Let Fortune lay on me her worst disgrace;
  Let folke orecharg'd with braine against me crie;
Let clouds bedimme my face, breake in mine eye;
  Let me no steps but of lost labour trace;
Let all the earth with scorne recount my case,
  But do not will me from my love to flie.
I do not enuie Aristotless wit,
  Nor do aspire to Cæsars bleeding fame;
Nor ought do care though some aboue me sit;
  Nor hope, nor wish another course to frame
    But that which once may win thy cruell hart:
    Thou art my wit, and thou my vertue art.

LXV

Love, by sure proofe I may call thee unkind,
  That giu'st no better ear to my iust cries;
Thou whom to me such good turnes should bind,
  As I may well recount, but none can prize:
For when, nak'd Boy, thou couldst no harbour finde
  In this old world, growne now so too, too wise,
I lodgd thee in my heart, and being blind
  By nature borne, I gaue to thee mine eyes;
Mine eyes! my light, my heart, my life, alas!
  If so great seruices may scorned be,
Yet let this thought thy Tygrish courage passe,
  That I perhaps am somewhat kinne to thee;
    Since in thine armes, if learnd fame truth hath spread,
    Thou bear'st the Arrow, I the Arrow-head.

LXVI

And do I see some cause a hope to feede,
  Or doth the tedious burden of long wo
In weaken'd minds quick apprehending breed
  Of euerie image which may comfort shew?
I cannot brag of word, much lesse of deed,
  Fortune wheeles still with me in one sort slow;
My wealth no more, and no whit lesse my need;
  Desier still on stilts of Feare doth go.
And yet amid all feares a hope there is,
  Stolne to my hart since last faire night, nay day,
Stellas eyes sent to me the beames of blisse,
  Looking on me while I lookt other way:
    But when mine eyes backe to their heau'n did moue,
    They fled with blush which guiltie seem'd of love.

LXVII

Hope, art thou true, or doest thou flatter me?
  Doth Stella now beginne with piteous eye
The ruines of her conquest to espie?
  Will she take time before all wracked be?
Her eyes-speech is translated thus by thee,
  But failst thou not in phrases so heau'nly hye?
Looke on againe, the faire text better prie;
  What blushing notes dost thou in Margent see?
What sighes stolne out, or kild before full-borne?
  Hast thou found such and such-like arguments,
Or art thou else to comfort me forsworne?
  Well, how-so thou interpret the contents,
    I am resolu'd thy errour to maintaine,
    Rather then by more truth to get more paine.

LXVIII

Stella, the onely planet of my light,
  Light of my life, and life of my desire,
Chiefe good whereto my hope doth only aspire,
  World of my wealth, and heau'n of my delight;
Why dost thou spend the treasures of thy sprite
  With voice more fit to wed Amphions lyre,
Seeking to quench in me the noble fire
  Fed by thy worth, and kindled by thy sight?
And all in vaine: for while thy breath most sweet
  With choisest words, thy words with reasons rare,
Thy reasons firmly set on Vertues feet,
  Labour to kill in me this killing care:
    O thinke I then, what paradise of ioy
    It is, so faire a vertue to enioy!

LXIX

O ioy to high for my low stile to show!
  O blisse fit for a nobler seat then me!
Enuie, put out thine eyes, least thou do see
  What oceans of delight in me do flowe!
My friend, that oft saw through all maskes my wo,
  Come, come, and let me powre my selfe on thee.
Gone is the Winter of my miserie!
  My Spring appeares; O see what here doth grow:
For Stella hath, with words where faith doth shine,
  Of her high heart giu'n me the Monarchie:
I, I, O I, may say that she is mine!
  And though she giue but thus conditionly,
    This realme of blisse while vertuous course I take,
    No kings be crown'd but they some couenants make.

LXX

My Muse may well grudge at my heau'nly ioy,
  Yf still I force her in sad rimes to creepe:
She oft hath drunk my teares, now hopes to enioy
  Nectar of mirth, since I Ioues cup do keepe.
Sonets be not bound Prentice to annoy;
  Trebles sing high, so well as bases deepe;
Griefe but Loves winter-liuerie is; the boy
  Hath cheekes to smile, so well as eyes to weepe.
Come then, my Muse, shew thou height of delight
  In well-raisde notes; my pen, the best it may,
Shall paint out ioy, though in but blacke and white.
  Cease, eager Muse; peace, pen, for my sake stay,
    I giue you here my hand for truth of this,
    Wise silence is best musicke unto blisse.

LXXI

Who will in fairest booke of Nature know
  How vertue may best lodg'd in Beautie be,
Let him but learne of Love to reade in thee,
  Stella, those faire lines which true goodnesse show.
There shall he find all vices ouerthrow,
  Not by rude force, but sweetest soueraigntie
Of reason, from whose light those night-birds flie,
  That inward sunne in thine eyes shineth so.
And, not content to be Perfections heire
  Thy selfe, doest striue all minds that way to moue,
Who marke in thee what is in thee most faire:
  So while thy beautie drawes the heart to love,
    As fast thy vertue bends that love to good:
    But, ah, Desire still cries, Giue me some food.

LXXII

Desire, though thou my old companion art,
   And oft so clings to my pure love that I
One from the other scarcely can discrie,
   While each doth blowe the fier of my hart;
Now from thy fellowship I needs must part;
   Venus is taught with Dians wings to flie;
I must no more in thy sweet passions lie;
   Vertues gold must now head my Cupids dart.
Seruice and honour, wonder with delight,
   Feare to offend, will worthie to appeare,
Care shining in mine eyes, faith in my sprite;
   These things are left me by my onely Deare:
      But thou, Desire, because thou wouldst haue all,
      Now banisht art; but yet, alas, how shall?

Second Song

Haue I caught my heau'nly iewell,
Teaching Sleepe most faire to be!
Now will I teach her that she,
When she wakes, is too-too cruell.

Since sweet Sleep her eyes hath charmed,
The two only darts of Love,
Now will I, with that Boy, proue,
Some play, while he is disamed.

Her tongue, waking, still refuseth,
Giuing frankly niggard no:
Now will I attempt to know
What no her tongue, sleeping, vseth.

See the hand that, waking, gardeth,
Sleeping, grants a free resort:
Now I will inuade the fort,
Cowards Love with losse rewardeth.

But, O foole, thinke of the danger
Of her iust and high disdaine;
Now will I, alas, refraine;
Love feares nothing else but anger.

Yet those lips, so sweetly swelling,
Do inuite a stealing kisse.
Now will I but venture this;
Who will reade, must first learne spelling.

Oh, sweet kisse! but ah, shes waking!
Lowring beautie chastens me:
Now will I for feare hence flee;
Foole, more Foole for no more taking.

LXXIII

Love, still a Boy, and oft a wanton is,
   School'd onely by his mothers tender eye;
What wonder then if he his lesson misse,
   When for so soft a rodde deare play he trye?
And yet my Starre, because a sugred kisse
   In sport I suckt while she asleepe did lye,
Doth lowre, nay chide, nay threat for only this.
   Sweet, it was saucie Love, not humble I.
But no scuse serues; she makes her wrath appeare
   In beauties throne: see now, who dares come neare
Those scarlet Iudges, thretning bloudie paine.
   O heau'nly foole, thy most kisse-worthy face
     Anger inuests with such a lovely grace,
     That Angers selfe I needs must kisse againe.

LXXIV

I neuer dranke of Aganippe well,
  Nor euer did in shade of Tempe sit,
And Muses scorne with vulgar brains to dwell;
  Poore Layman I, for sacred rites unfit.
Some doe I heare of Poets fury tell,
  But, God wot, wot not what they meane by it;
And this I sweare by blackest brooke of hell,
  I am no pick-purse of anothers wit.
How falles it then, that with so smooth an ease
  My thoughts I speake; and what I speake doth flow
In verse, and that my verse best wits doth please?
  Ghesse we the cause? What, is it this? Fie, no.
    Or so? Much lesse. How then? Sure thus it is,
    My lips are sweet, inspir'd with Stellas kisse.

LXXV

Of all the Kings that euer here did raigne,
   Edward, nam'd fourth, as first in praise I name:
Not for his faire outside, nor well-lin'd braine,
   Although lesse gifts impe feathers oft on fame.
Nor that he could, young-wise, wise-valiant, frame
   His sires reuenge, ioyn'd with a kingdomes gaine;
And gain'd by Mars, could yet mad Mars so tame,
   That balance weigh'd, what sword did late obtaine.
Nor that he made the floure-de-luce so 'fraid,
   (Though strongly hedg'd) of bloudy lyons pawes,
That wittie Lewes to him a tribute paid:
   Nor this, nor that, nor any such small cause;
     But only for this worthy King durst proue
     To lose his crowne, rather than faile his love.

LXXVI

She comes, and streight therewith her shining twins do
moue
  Their rayes to me, who in their tedious absence lay
Benighted in cold wo; but now appears my day,
  The only light of ioy, the only warmth of love.
She comes with light and warmth, which, like Aurora,
proue
  Of gentle force, so that mine eyes dare gladly play
With such a rosie Morne, whose beames, most freshly gay,
  Scorch not, but onely doe dark chilling sprites remoue.
But lo, while I do speake, it groweth noone with me,
  Her flamie-glistring lights increse with time and place,
My heart cries, oh! it burnes, mine eyes now dazl'd be;
  No wind, no shade can coole: what helpe then in my case?
    But with short breath, long looks, staid feet, and aching
hed,
    Pray that my Sunne goe downe with meeker beames to
bed.

LXXVII

Those lookes, whose beames be ioy, whose motion is
                                    delight;
  That face, whose lecture shews what perfect beauty is;
That presence, which doth giue darke hearts a liuing light;
  That grace, which Venus weeps that she her selfe doth
                                    misse;
That hand, which without touch holds more then Atlas
                                    might;
  Those lips, which make deaths pay a meane price for a
                                    kisse;
That skin, whose passe-praise hue scornes this poor tearm
                                    of white;
  Those words, which do sublime the quintessence of bliss;
That voyce, which makes the soule plant himselfe in the
                                    ears,
  That conuersation sweet, where such high comforts be,
As, consterd in true speech, the name of heaun it beares;
  Makes me in my best thoughts and quietst iudgments see
    That in no more but these I might be fully blest:
    Yet, ah, my mayd'n Muse doth blush to tell the best.

LXXVIII

O how the pleasant ayres of true love be
  Infected by those vapours which arise
From out that noysome gulfe, which gaping lies
  Betweene the iawes of hellish Ielousie!
A monster, others harme, selfe-miserie,
  Beauties plague, Vertues scourge, succour of lies;
Who his owne ioy to his owne hurt applies,
  And onely cherish doth with iniurie:
Who since he hath, by Natures speciall grace,
  So piercing pawes as spoyle when they embrace;
So nimble feet as stirre still, though on thornes;
  So many eyes, ay seeking their owne woe;
    So ample eares as neuer good newes know:
    Is it not euill that such a deuil wants hornes?

LXXIX

Sweet kisse, thy sweets I faine would sweetly endite,
    Which, euen of sweetnesse sweetest sweetner art;
Pleasingst consort, where each sence holds a part;
    Which, coupling Doues, guides Venus chariot right.
Best charge, and brauest retrait in Cupids fight;
    A double key, which opens to the heart,
Most rich when most riches it impart;
    Nest of young ioyes, Schoolemaster of delight,
Teaching the meane at once to take and giue;
    The friendly fray, where blowes both wound and heale,
The prettie death, while each in other liue.
    Poore hopes first wealth, ostage of promist weale;
      Breakfast of love. But lo, lo, where she is,
      Cease we to praise; now pray we for a kisse.

LXXX

Sweet-swelling lip, well maist thou swell in pride,
　Since best wits thinke it wit thee to admire;
Natures praise, Vertues stall; Cupids cold fire,
　Whence words, not words but heau'nly graces slide;
The new Parnassus, where the Muses bide;
　Sweetner of Musicke, Wisedomes beautifier,
Breather of life, and fastner of desire,
　Where Beauties blush in Honors graine is dide.
Thus much my heart compeld my mouth to say;
　But now, spite of my heart, my mouth will stay,
Loathing all lies, doubting this flatterie is:
　And no spurre can his resty race renewe,
　　Without, how farre this praise is short of you,
　　Sweet Lipp, you teach my mouth with one sweet kisse.

LXXXI

O kisse, which dost those ruddie gemmes impart,
  Or gemmes or fruits of new-found Paradise,
Breathing all blisse, and sweetning to the heart,
  Teaching dumbe lips a nobler exercise;
O kisse, which soules, euen soules, together ties
  By linkes of love and only Natures art,
How faine would I paint thee to all mens eyes.
  Or of thy gifts at least shade out some part!
But she forbids; with blushing words she sayes
  She builds her fame on higher-seated praise.
But my heart burnes; I cannot silent be.
    Then, since, dear life, you faine would haue me peace,
      And I, mad with delight, want wit to cease,
      Stop you my mouth with still still kissing me.

LXXXII

Nymph of the garden where all beauties be,
   Beauties which do in excellencie passe
His who till death lookt in a watrie glasse,
   Or hers whom nakd the Troian boy did see;
Sweet-gard'n-nymph, which keepes the Cherrie-tree
   Whose fruit doth farre the Hesperian tast surpasse,
Most sweet-faire, most faire-sweete, do not, alas,
   From comming neare those Cherries banish mee.
For though, full of desire, empty of wit,
   Admitted late by your best-graced grace,
I caught at one of them, and hungry bit;
   Pardon that fault; once more grant me the place;
    And I do sweare, euen by the same delight,
    I will but kisse; I neuer more will bite.

LXXXIII

Good brother Philip, I haue borne you long;
   I was content you should in fauour creepe,
While craftely you seem'd your cut to keepe,
   As though that faire soft hand did you great wrong:
I bare with enuie, yet I bare your song,
   When in her necke you did love-ditties peepe;
Nay (more foole I) oft suffred you to sleepe
   In lillies neast where Loves selfe lies along.
What, doth high place ambitious thoughts augment?
   Is sawcinesse reward of curtesie?
Cannot such grace your silly selfe content,
   But you must needs with those lips billing be,
     And through those lips drinke nectar from that toong?
     Leaue that, Syr Phip, least off your neck be wroong!

Third Song

If Orpheus voyce had force to breathe such musickes love
Through pores of senceles trees, as it could make them
                              moue;
If stones good measure daunc'd, the Theban walles to build
To cadence of the tunes which Amphions lyre did yeeld;
More cause a like effect at least-wise bringeth:
O stones, O trees, learne hearing,--Stella singeth.

If love might sweeten so a boy of shepheard brood,
To make a lyzard dull, to taste loves dainty food;
If eagle fierce could so in Grecian mayde delight,
As her eyes were his light, her death his endlesse night,
Earth gaue that love; heau'n, I trow, love refineth,
O birds, O beasts, looke love (lo) Stella shineth.

The beasts, birds, stones, and trees feele this, and, feeling,
                              love;
And if the trees nor stones stirre not the same to proue,
Nor beasts nor birds do come unto this blessed gaze,
Know that small love is quicke, and great love doth amaze;
They are amaz'd, but you with reason armed,
O eyes, O eares of men, how you are charmed!

LXXXIV

High way, since you my chiefe Pernassus be,
  And that my Muse, to some eares not unsweet,
Tempers her words to trampling horses feete
  More oft then to a chamber-melodie.
Now, blessed you beare onward blessed me
  To her, where I my heart, safe-left, shall meet;
My Muse and I must you of dutie greet
  With thankes and wishes, wishing thankfully.
Be you still faire, honord by publicke heede;
  By no encroachment wrong'd, nor time forgot;
Nor blam'd for bloud, nor sham'd for sinfull deed;
  And that you know I enuy you no lot
    Of highest wish, I wish you so much bliss,
    Hundreds of yeares you Stellaes feet may kisse.

LXXXV

I see the house, (my heart thy selfe containe!)
   Beware full sailes drowne not thy tottring barge,
Least ioy, by nature apt sprites to enlarge,
   Thee to thy wracke beyond thy limits straine;
Nor do like Lords whose weake confused braine
   Not 'pointing to fit folkes each undercharge,
While euerie office themselues will discharge,
   With doing all, leaue nothing done but paine.
But giue apt seruants their due place: let eyes
   See beauties totall summe summ'd in her face;
Let eares heare speach which wit to wonder ties;
   Let breath sucke vp those sweetes; let armes embrace
     The globe of weale, lips Loves indentures make;
     Thou but of all the kingly tribute take.

Fourth Song.

Onely Ioy, now here you are,
Fit to heare and ease my care,
Let my whispering voyce obtaine
Sweete reward for sharpest paine;
Take me to thee, and thee to mee:
No, no, no, no, my Deare, let bee.

Night hath closde all in her cloke,
Twinkling starres love-thoughts prouoke,
Danger hence, good care doth keepe,
Iealouzie hemselfe doth sleepe;
Take me to thee, and thee to mee:
No, no, no, no, my Deare, let bee.

Better place no wit can finde,
Cupids knot to loose or binde;
These sweet flowers our fine bed too,
Vs in their best language woo:
Take me to thee, and thee to mee:
No, no, no, no, my Deare, let bee.

This small light the moone bestowes
Serues thy beames but to disclose;
So to raise my hap more hie,
Feare not else, none vs can spie;
Take me to thee, and thee to mee:
No, no, no, no, my Deare, let bee.

That you heard was but a mouse,
Dumbe Sleepe holdeth all the house:
Yet asleepe, me thinkes they say,

Yong fooles take time while you may;
Take me to thee, and thee to mee:
No, no, no, no, my Deare, let bee.

Niggard time threates, if we misse
This large offer of our blisse,
Long stay, ere he graunt the same:
Sweet, then, while ech thing doth frame,
Take me to thee, and thee to mee:
No, no, no, no, my Deare, let bee.

Your faire Mother is abed,
Candles out and curtaines spred;
She thinkes you do letters write;
Write, but first let me endite;
Take me to thee, and thee to mee:
No, no, no, no, my Deare, let bee.

Sweete, alas, why striue you thus?
Concord better fitteth vs;
Leaue to Mars the force of hands,
Your power in your beautie stands;
Take me to thee, and thee to mee:
No, no, no, no, my Deare, let bee.

Wo to mee, and do you sweare
Me to hate, but I forbeare?
Cursed be my destines all,
That brought me so high to fall;
Soone with my death I will please thee:
No, no, no, no, my Deare, let bee.

LXXXVI

Alas, whence came this change of lookes? If I
   Haue chang'd desert, let mine owne conscience be
A still-felt plague to selfe-condemning mee;
   Let woe gripe on my heart, shame loade mine eye:
But if all faith, like spotlesse Ermine, ly
   Safe in my soule, which only doth to thee,
As his sole obiect of felicitie,
   With wings of love in aire of wonder flie,
O ease your hand, treate not so hard your slaue;
   In iustice paines come not till faults do call:
Or if I needs, sweet Iudge, must torments haue,
   Vse something else to chasten me withall
     Then those blest eyes, where all my hopes do dwell:
     No doome should make ones Heau'n become his Hell.

Fifth Song

While fauour fed my hope, delight with hope was brought,
Thought waited on delight, and speech did follow thought;
Then grew my tongue and pen records unto thy glory,
I thought all words were lost that were not spent of thee,
I thought each place was darke but where thy lights would
be,
And all eares worse than deaf that heard not out thy storie.

I said thou wert most faire, and so indeed thou art;
I said thou wert most sweet, sweet poison to my heart;
I said my soule was thine, O that I then had lyed;
I said thine eyes were starres, thy breast the milken way,
Thy fingers Cupids shafts, thy voyce the angels lay:
And all I said so well, as no man it denied.

But now that hope is lost, unkindnesse kils delight;
Yet thought and speech do liue, though metamorphos'd
quite,
For rage now rules the raines which guided were by
pleasure;
I thinke now of thy faults, who late thought of thy praise,
That speech falles now to blame, which did thy honour
raise,
The same key open can, which can lock vp a treasure.

Then thou, whom partiall heauens conspird in one to
frame
The proofe of Beauties worth, th'inheritrix of fame,
The mansion seat of blisse, and iust excuse of lovers;
See now those feathers pluckt, wherewith thou flew'st most
high:

See what cloudes of reproach shall dark thy honours skie:
Whose owne fault cast him downe hardly high state
                            recouers.

And, O my muse, though oft you luld her in your lap,
And then a heau'nly Child, gaue her Ambrosian pap,
And to that braine of hers your kindest gifts infused;
Since she, disdaining me, doth you in me disdaine,
Suffer not her to laugh, while both we suffer paine.
Princes in subiects wrong must deeme themselues abused.

Your client, poore my selfe, shall Stella handle so!
Reuenge! revenge! my Muse! defiance trumpet blow;
Threaten what may be done, yet do more then you
                            threaten;
Ah, my sute granted is, I feele my breast doth swell;
No, child, a lesson new you shall begin to spell,
Sweet babes must babies haue, but shrewd gyrles must be
                            beaten.

Thinke now no more to heare of warme fine-odour'd snow,
Nor blushing Lillies, nor pearles Ruby-hidden row,
Nor of that golden sea, whose waues in curles are broken,
But of thy soule, so fraught with such ungratefulnesse,
As where thou soone might'st helpe, most faith dost most
                            oppresse;
Ungratefull, who is cald, the worst of euils is spoken,

Yet worse then worst, I say thou art a Theefe, A theefe!
Now God forbid! a theefe! and of wurst theeues the cheefe:
Theeues steal for need, and steale but goods which paine
                            recouers,
But thou, rich in all ioyes, dost rob my ioyes from me,
Which cannot be restord by time or industrie:
Of foes the spoyle is euill, far worse of constant lovers.

Yet--gentle English theeues do rob, but will not slay,
Thou English murdring theefe, wilt haue harts for thy prey:
The name of murdrer now on thy faire forehead sitteth,
And euen while I do speake, my death wounds bleeding be,
Which, I protest, proceed from only cruell thee:
Who may, and will not saue, murder in truth committeth.

But murder, priuate fault, seemes but a toy to thee:
I lay then to thy charge uniustest tyrannie,
If rule by force, without all claim, a Tyran showeth;
For thou dost lord my heart, who am not borne thy slaue,
And, which is worse, makes me, most guiltlesse, torments
                                        haue:
A rightfull prince by unright deeds a Tyran groweth.

Lo, you grow proud with this, for Tyrans make folke bow:
Of foule rebellion then I do appeach thee now,
Rebell by Natures law, rebell by law of Reason:
Thou, sweetest subiect wert, borne in the realme of Love,
And yet against thy prince thy force dost daily proue:
No vertue merits praise, once toucht with blot of Treason.

But valiant Rebels oft in fooles mouths purchase fame:
I now then staine thy white with vagabonding shame,
Both rebell to the sonne and vagrant from the mother;
For wearing Venus badge in euery part of thee,
Unto Dianaes traine thou, runnaway, didst flie:
Who faileth one is false, though trusty to another.

What, is not this enough! nay, farre worse commeth here;
A witch, I say, thou art, though thou so faire appeare;
For, I protest, my sight neuer thy face enioyeth,
But I in me am chang'd, I am aliue and dead,
My feete are turn'd to rootes, my hart becommeth lead:
No witchcraft is so euill as which mans mind destroyeth.

Yet witches may repent; thou art farre worse then they:
Alas that I am forst such euill of thee to say:
I say thou art a diuell, though cloth'd in angels shining;
For thy face tempts my soule to leaue the heauens for thee,
And thy words of refuse do powre euen hell on mee:
Who tempt, and tempting plague, are diuels in true
                                    defining.

You, then, ungrateful theefe, you murdring Tyran, you,
You rebell runaway, to lord and lady untrue,
You witch, you Diuell (alas) you still of me beloved,
You see what I can say; mend yet your froward mind,
And such skill in my Muse, you, reconcil'd, shall find,
That all these cruell words your praises shalbe proued.

Sixth Song

O you that heare this voice,
O you that see this face,
Say whether of the choice
Deserues the former place:
Feare not to iudge this bate,
For it is void of hate.

This side doth Beauty take.
For that doth Musike speake;
Fit Oratours to make
The strongest iudgements weake:
The barre to plead their right
Is only true delight.

Thus doth the voice and face,
These gentle Lawiers, wage,
Like loving brothers case,
For fathers heritage;
That each, while each contends,
It selfe to other lends.

For Beautie beautifies
With heau'nly hew and grace
The heau'nly harmonies;
And in this faultlesse face
The perfect beauties be
A perfect harmony.

Musick more loftly swels
In speeches nobly plac'd;
Beauty as farre excels,

In action aptly grac'd:
A friend each party draws
To countenance his cause.

Love more affected seemes
To Beauties lovely light;
And Wonder more esteemes
Of Musickes wondrous might;
But both to both so bent,
As both in both are spent.

Musicke doth witnesse call
The eare his truth to trie;
Beauty brings to the hall
Eye-iudgement of the eye:
Both in their obiects such,
As no exceptions tutch.

The common sense, which might
Be arbiter of this,
To be, forsooth, vpright,
To both sides partiall is;
He layes on this chiefe praise,
Chiefe praise on that he laies.

Then reason, princesse hy,
Whose throne is in the minde,
Which Musicke can in sky
And hidden beauties finde,
Say whether thou wilt crowne
With limitlesse renowne?

Seuenth Song

Whose senses in so euill consort their stepdame Nature
                                        laies,
That rauishing delight in them most sweete tunes do not
                                        raise;
Or if they do delight therein, yet are so closde with wit,
As with ententious lips to set a title vaine on it;
O let them heare these sacred tunes, and learne in Wonders
                                        scholes,
To be, in things past bounds of wit, fooles: if they be not
                                        fooles.

Who haue so leaden eyes, as not to see sweet Beauties
                                        show,
Or, seeing, haue so wooden wits, as not that worth to
                                        know,
Or, knowing, haue so muddy minds, as not to be in love,
Or, loving, haue so frothy thoughts, as eas'ly thence to
                                        moue;
O let them see these heau'nly beames, and in faire letters
                                        reede
A lesson fit, both sight and skill, love and firme love to
                                        breede.

Heare then, but then with wonder heare, see, but adoring,
                                        see,
No mortall gifts, no earthly fruites, now here descended be:
See, doo you see this face? a face, nay, image of the skies,
Of which the two life-giuing lights are figur'd in her eyes:
Heare you this soule-inuading voice, and count it but a
                                        voice?
The very essence of their tunes, when angels do reioyce.

Eighth Song

In a groue most rich of shade,
Where birds wanton musicke made,
Maie, then yong, his pide weedes showing,
New-perfum'd with flowers fresh growing:

Astrophel with Stella sweet
Did for mutual comfort meete,
Both within themselues oppressed,
But each in the other blessed.

Him great harmes had taught much care,
Her faire necke a foule yoke bare;
But her sight his cares did banish,
In his sight her yoke did vanish:

Wept they had, alas, the while,
But now teares themselues did smile,
While their eyes, by Love directed,
Enterchangeably reflected.

Sigh they did; but now betwixt
Sighes of woe were glad sighes mixt;
With arms crost, yet testifying
restlesse rest, and liuing dying.

Their eares hungrie of each word
Which the deare tongue would afford;
But their tongues restrain'd from walking,
Till their harts had ended talking.

But when their tongues could not speake,
Love it selfe did silence breake;
Love did set his lips asunder,
Thus to speake in love and wonder.

Stella, Soueraigne of my ioy,
Faire triumpher of annoy;
Stella, Starre of heauenly fier,
Stella, loadstar of desier;

Stella, in whose shining eyes
Are the lights of Cupids skies,
Whose beames, where they once are darted,
Love therewith is streight imparted;

Stella, whose voice when it speakes
Senses all asunder breakes;
Stella, whose voice, when it singeth,
Angels to acquaintance bringeth;

Stella, in whose body is
Writ each caracter of blisse;
Whose face all, all beauty passeth,
Saue thy mind, which it surpasseth.

Graunt, O graunt; but speach, alas,
Failes me, fearing on to passe:
Graunt, O me: what am I saying?
But no fault there is in praying.

Graunt (O Deere) on knees I pray,
(Knees on ground he then did stay)
That, not I, but since I love you,
Time and place for me may moue you.

Neuer season was more fit;
Never roome more apt for it;
Smiling ayre allowes my reason;
These birds sing, Now vse the season.

This small wind, which so sweete is,
See how it the leaues doth kisse;
Each tree in his best attiring,
Sense of Love to Love inspiring.

Love makes earth the water drink,
Love to earth makes water sinke;
And, if dumbe things be so witty,
Shall a heauenly Grace want pitty?

There his hands, in their speech, faine
Would haue made tongues language plaine;
But her hands, his hands repelling,
Gaue repulse all grace expelling.

Then she spake; her speech was such,
So not eares, but hart did tuch:
While such-wise she love denied,
And yet love she signified.

Astrophel, sayd she, my love,
Cease, in these effects, to proue;
Now be still, yet still beleeue me,
Thy griefe more then death would grieue me.

If that any thought in me
Can tast comfort but of thee,
Let me, fed with hellish anguish,
Ioylesse, hopelesse, endlesse languish.

If those eyes you praised be
Halfe so deare as you to me,
Let me home returne, starke blinded
Of those eyes, and blinder minded;

If to secret of my hart,
I do any wish impart,
Where thou art not formost placed,
Be both wish and I defaced.

If more may be sayd, I say,
All my blisse in thee I lay;
If thou love, my love, content thee,
For all love, all faith is meant thee.

Trust me, while I thee deny,
In my selfe the smart I try;
Tyran Honour doth thus vse thee,
Stellas selfe might not refuse thee.

Therefore, deare, this no more moue,
Least, though I leaue not thy love,
Which too deep in me is framed,
I should blush when thou art named.

Therewithall away she went,
Leauing him to passion rent,
With what she had done and spoken,
That therewith my song is broken.

Ninth Song.

Go, my Flocke, go, get you hence,
Seeke a better place of feeding,
Where you may haue some defence
Fro the stormes in my breast breeding,
And showers from mine eyes proceeding.

Leaue a wretch, in whom all wo
Can abide to keepe no measure;
Merry Flocke, such one forego,
Unto whom mirth is displeasure,
Onely rich in mischiefs treasure.

Yet, alas, before you go,
Heare your wofull Maisters story,
Which to stones I els would show:
Sorrow only then hath glory
When 'tis excellently sorry.

Stella, fiercest shepherdesse,
Fiercest, but yet fairest euer;
Stella, whom, O heauens still blesse,
Though against me she perseuer,
Though I blisse enherit neuer:

Stella hath refused me!
Stella, who more love hath proued,
In this caitife heart to be,
Then can in good eawes be moued
Toward Lambkins best beloved.

Stella hath refused me!
Astrophell, that so well served
In this pleasant Spring must see,
While in pride flowers be preserued,
Himselfe onely Winter-sterued.

Why (alas) doth she then sweare
That she loveth me so dearely,
Seeing me so long to beare
Coles of love that burne so cleerly,
And yet leaue me helplesse meerely?

Is that love? forsooth, I trow,
If I saw my good dog grieued,
And a helpe for him did know,
My love should not be beleeued,
But he were by me releeued.

No, she hates me, well-away,
Faining love, somewhat to please me:
For she knows, if she display
All her hate, death soone would seaze me,
And of hideous torments ease me.

Then adieu, deare Flocke, adieu;
But, alas, if in your straying
Heauenly Stella meete with you,
Tell her, in your pitious blaying,
Her poore Slaues uniust decaying.

LXXXVII

When I was forst from Stella euer deere,
  Stella, food of my thoughts, hart of my hart;
Stella, whose eyes make all my tempests cleere,
  By Stellas lawes of duetie to depart;
Alas, I found that she with me did smart;
  I saw that teares did in her eyes appeare;
I sawe that sighes her sweetest lips did part,
  And her sad words my sadded sense did heare.
For me, I wept to see pearles scatter'd so;
  I sigh'd her sighes, and wailed for her wo;
Yet swam in ioy, such love in her was seene.
  Thus, while th' effect most bitter was to me,
    And nothing then the cause more sweet could be,
    I had bene vext, if vext I had not beene.

LXXXVIII

Out, traytor Absence, dar'st thou counsell me
  From my deare captainesse to run away,
Because in braue array heere marcheth she,
  That, to win mee, oft shewes a present pay?
Is faith so weake? or is such force in thee?
  When sun is hid, can starres such beames display?
Cannot heau'ns food, once felt, keepe stomakes free
  From base desire on earthly cates to pray?
Tush, Absence; while thy mistes eclipse that light,
  My orphan sense flies to the inward sight,
Where memory sets forth the beames of love;
  That, where before hart lov'd and eyes did see,
    In hart both sight and love now coupled be:
    United powers make each the stronger proue.

LXXXIX

Now that of absence the most irksom night
  With darkest shade doth ouercome my day;
Since Stellaes eyes, wont to giue me my day,
  Leauing my hemisphere, leaue me in night;
Each day seemes long, and longs for long-staid night;
  The night, as tedious, wooes th' approch of day:
Tired with the dusty toiles of busie day,
  Languisht with horrors of the silent night,
Suff'ring the euils both of day and night,
  While no night is more darke then is my day,
Nor no day hath lesse quiet then my night:
  With such bad-mixture of my night and day,
    That liuing thus in blackest Winter night,
    I feele the flames of hottest Sommer day.

XC

Stella, thinke not that I by verse seeke fame,
  Who seeke, who hope, who love, who liue but thee;
Thine eyes my pride, thy lips mine history:
  If thou praise not, all other praise is shame.
Nor so ambitious am I, as to frame
  A nest for my young praise in lawrell tree:
In truth, I sweare I wish not there should be
  Grau'd in my epitaph a Poets name.
Ne, if I would, could I iust title make,
  That any laud thereof to me should growe,
Without my plumes from others wings I take:
  For nothing from my wit or will doth flow,
    Since all my words thy beauty doth endite,
    And Love doth hold my hand, and makes me write.

XCI

Stella, while now, by Honours cruell might,
  I am from you, light of my life, misled,
And whiles, faire you, my sunne, thus ouerspred
  With Absence vaile, I liue in Sorrowes night;
If this darke place yet shewe like candle-light,
  Some beauties peece, as amber-colour'd hed,
Milke hands, rose cheeks, or lips more sweet, more red;
  Or seeing jets blacke but in blacknesse bright;
They please, I do confesse they please mine eyes.
  But why? because of you they models be;
Models, such be wood-globes of glist'ring skies.
  Deere therefore be not iaelous ouer me,
    If you heare that they seeme my heart to moue;
    Not them, O no, but you in them I love.

XCII

Be your words made, good Sir, of Indian ware,
   That you allow me them by so small rate?
Or do you curtted Spartanes imitate?
   Or do you meane my tender eares to spare,
That to my questions you so totall are?
   When I demaund of Phoenix-Stellas state,
You say, forsooth, you left her well of late:
   O God, thinke you that satisfies my care?
I would know whether she did sit or walke;
   How cloth'd; how waited on; sigh'd she, or smilde
Whereof, with whom, how often did she talke;
   With what pastimes Times iourney she beguilde;
     If her lips daignd to sweeten my poore name.
     Saie all; and all well sayd, still say the same.

Tenth Song

O deare Life, when shall it bee
That mine eyes thine eyes shall see,
And in them thy mind discouer
Whether absence haue had force
Thy remembrance to diuorce
From the image of thy lover?

Or if I my self find not,
After parting aught forgot,
Nor debar'd from Beauties treasure,
Let not tongue aspire to tell
In what high ioyes I shall dwell;
Only thought aymes at the pleasure.

Thought, therefore, I will send thee
To take vp the place for me:
Long I will not after tary,
There unseene, thou mayst be bold,
Those faire wonders to behold,
Which in them my hopes do cary.

Thought, see thou no place forbeare,
Enter brauely euerywhere,
Seize on all to her belonging;
But if thou wouldst garded be,
Fearing her beames, take with thee
Strength of liking, rage of longing.

Thinke of that most gratefull time
When my leaping heart will climb,
In thy lips to haue his biding,

There those roses for to kisse,
Which do breathe a sugred blisse,
Opening rubies, pearles diuiding.

Thinke of my most princely power,
Which I blessed shall deuow'r
With my greedy licorous sences,
Beauty, musicke, sweetnesse, love,
While she doth against me proue
Her strong darts but weake defences.

Thinke, thinke of those dalyings,
When with doue-like murmurings,
With glad moning, passed anguish,
We change eyes, and hart for hart,
Each to other do depart,
Ioying till ioy makes vs languish.

O my Thoughts, my Thoughts surcease,
Thy delights my woes increse,
My life melts with too much thinking;
Thinke no more, but die in me,
Till thou shalt reuiued be,
At her lips my Nectar drinking.

XCIII

O fate, O fault, O curse, child of my blisse!
  What sobs can giue words grace my griefe to show?
What inke is blacke inough to paint my woe?
  Through me (wretch me) euen Stella vexed is.
Yet, Trueth, if Caitiues breath may call thee, this
  Witnesse with me, that my foule stumbling so,
From carelessenesse did in no maner grow;
  But wit, confus'd with too much care, did misse.
And do I, then, my selfe this vaine scuse giue?
  I haue (liue I, and know this) harmed thee;
Tho' worlds 'quite me, shall I my selfe forgiue?
  Only with paines my paines thus eased be,
    That all thy hurts in my harts wracke I reede;
    I cry thy sighs, my deere, thy teares I bleede.

XCIV

Griefe, find the words; for thou hast made my braine
   So darke with misty vapuors, which arise
From out thy heauy mould, that inbent eyes
   Can scarce discerne the shape of mine owne paine.
Do thou, then (for thou canst) do thou complaine
   For my poore soule, which now that sicknesse tries,
Which euen to sence, sence of it selfe denies,
   Though harbengers of death lodge there his traine.
Or if thy love of plaint yet mine forbeares,
   As of a Caitife worthy so to die;
Yet waile thy selfe, and waile with causefull teares,
   That though in wretchednesse thy life doth lie,
      Yet growest more wretched then by nature beares
      By being plac'd in such a wretch as I.

XCV

Yet sighes, deare sighs, indeede true friends you are,
  That do not leaue your best friend at the wurst,
But, as you with my breast I oft haue nurst,
  So, gratefull now, you waite upon my care.
Faint coward Ioy no longer tarry dare,
  Seeing Hope yeeld when this wo strake him furst;
Delight exclaims he is for my fault curst,
  Though oft himselfe my mate in Armes he sware;
Nay, Sorrow comes with such maine rage, that he
  Kils his owne children (teares) finding that they
By Love were made apt to consort with me.
  Only, true Sighs, you do not goe away:
    Thanke may you haue for such a thankfull part,
    Thank-worthiest yet when you shall break my hart.

XCVI

Thought, with good cause thou lik'st so well the night,
  Since kind or chance giues both one liuerie,
Both sadly blacke, both blackly darkned be;
  Night bard from Sunne, thou from thy owne sunlight;
Silence in both displaies his sullen might;
  Slow heauinesse in both holds one degree
That full of doubts, thou of perplexity;
  Thy teares expresse Nights natiue moisture right;
In both amazeful solitarinesse:
  In night, of sprites, the gastly powers do stur;
In thee or sprites or sprited gastlinesse.
  But, but (alas) Nights side the ods hath fur:
    For that, at length, yet doth inuite some rest;
    Thou, though still tired, yet still doost it detest.

XCVII

Dian, that faine would cheare her friend the Night,
　Shewes her oft, at the full, her fairest face,
Bringing with her those starry Nymphs, whose chace
　From heau'nly standing hits each mortall wight.
But ah, poore Night, in love with Phoebus light,
　And endlesly dispairing of his grace,
Her selfe, to shewe no other ioy hath place;
　Sylent and sad, in mourning weedes doth dight.
Euen so (alas) a lady, Dians peere,
　With choise delights and rarest company
Would faine driue cloudes from out my heauy cheere;
　But, wo is me, though Ioy her selfe were she,
　　Shee could not shew my blind braine waies of ioy,
　　While I despaire my sunnes sight to enioy.

XCVIII

Ah, bed! the field where Ioyes peace some do see,
  The field where all my thoughts to warre be train'd,
How is thy grace by my strange fortune strain'd!
  How thy lee-shores by my sighes stormed be!
With sweete soft shades thou oft inuitest me
  To steale some rest; but, wretch, I am constrain'd,
Spurd with Loves spur, though gald, and shortly rain'd
  With Cares hard hand to turne and tosse in thee,
While the blacke horrors of the silent night
  Paint Woes blacke face so liuely to my sight
That tedious leasure markes each wrinkled line:
  But when Aurora leades out Phoebus daunce,
    Mine eyes then only winke; for spite, perchaunce,
    That wormes should haue their sun, & I want mine.

XCIX

When far-spent Night perswades each mortall eye,
   To whome nor Art nor Nature graunteth light,
To lay his then marke-wanting shafts of sight,
   Clos'd with their quiuers, in Sleeps armory;
With windowes ope, then most my mind doth lie,
   Viewing the shape of darknesse, and delight
Takes in that sad hue, which, with th' inward night
   Of his mazde powers, keepes perfet harmony:
But when birds charme, and that sweete aire which is
   Mornes messenger, with rose-enameld skies
Cals each wight to salute the floure of blisse;
   In tombe of lids then buried are mine eyes,
     Forst by their Lord, who is asham'd to find
     Such light in sense, with such a darkned mind.

C

O teares! no teares, but raine, from Beauties skies,
  Making those lillies and those roses growe,
Which ay most faire, now more then most faire shew,
  While gracefull Pitty Beautie beautifies.
O honied sighs! which from that breast do rise,
  Whose pants do make unspilling creame to flow,
Wing'd with whose breath, so pleasing Zephires blow.
  As might refresh the hell where my soule fries.
O plaints! conseru'd in such a sugred phrase,
  That Eloquence itself enuies your praise,
While sobd-out words a perfect musike giue.
  Such teares, sighs, plaints, no sorrow is, but ioy:
    Or if such heauenly signes must proue annoy,
    All mirth farewell, let me in sorrow liue.

CI

Stella is sicke, and in that sicke-bed lies
　Sweetnesse, which breathes and pants as oft as she:
And Grace, sicke too, such fine conclusion tries,
　That Sickenesse brags it selfe best grac'd to be.
Beauty is sicke, but sicke in so faire guise,
　That in that palenesse Beauties white we see;
And Ioy, which is inseparate from those eyes,
　Stella now learnes (strange case) to weepe in me.
Love mones thy paine, and like a faithfull page,
　As thy lookes sturre, runs vp and downe, to make
All folkes prest at thy will thy paine to swage;
　Nature with care sweates for hir darlings sake,
　　Knowing worlds passe, ere she enough can finde,
　　Of such heauen-stuffe to cloath so heau'nly minde.

CII

Where be those roses gone, which sweetned so our eyes?
  Where those red cheeks, which oft, with faire encrease,
                    did frame
The height of honour in the kindly badge of shame?
  Who hath the crimson weeds stolne from my morning
                    skies?
How doth the colour vade of those vermilion dies,
  Which Nature self did make, and self-ingrain'd the same?
I would know by what right this palenesse ouercame
  That hue whose force my hart still unto thraldome ties?
Galens adoptiue sonnes, who by a beaten way
  Their iudgements hackney on, the fault of sicknesse lay;
But feeling proofe makes me say they mistake it furre:
  It is but love which makes this paper perfit white,
    To write therein more fresh the storie of delight,
    Whiles Beauties reddest inke Venus for him doth sturre.

CIII

O happie Thames, that didst my Stella beare!
  I saw thee with full many a smiling line
Upon thy cheerefull face, Ioyes liuery weare,
  While those faire planets on thy streames did shine.
The boate for ioy could not to daunce forbear,
  While wanton winds, with beauties so diuine
Ravisht, staid not, till in her golden haire
  They did themselues (O sweetest prison) twine.
And faine those Æols youth there would their stay
  Haue made, but forst by Nature still to flie,
First did with puffing kisse those Lockes display:
  She, so disheuld blusht: from window I
    With sight thereof cride out, O faire disgrace,
    Let Honor selfe to thee grant highest place.

CIV

Enuious wits, what hath bene mine offence,
   That with such poysonous care my lookes you marke,
That to each word, nay sigh of mine, you harke,
   As grudging me my sorrowes eloquence?
Ah, is it not enough, that I am thence,
   Thence, so farre thence, that scantly any sparke
Of comfort dare come to this dungeon darke,
   Where Rigours exile lockes vp al my sense?
But if I by a happie window passe,
   If I but stars vppon mine armour beare;
Sicke, thirsty, glad (though but of empty glasse):
   Your morall notes straight my hid meaning teare
     From out my ribs, and, puffing, proues that I
     Doe Stella love: fooles, who doth it deny?

Eleuenth Song

Who is it that this darke night
Underneath my window playneth?
It is one who from thy sight
Being, ah exil'd, disdayneth
Euery other vulgar light.

Why, alas, and are you he?
Be not yet those fancies changed?
Deare, when you find change in me,
Though from me you be estranged,
Let my chaunge to ruin be.

Well, in absence this will dy;
Leaue to see, and leaue to wonder.
Absence sure will helpe, if I
Can learne how my selfe to sunder
From what in my hart doth ly.

But time will these thoughts remoue;
Time doth work what no man knoweth.
Time doth as the subiect proue;
With time still the affection groweth
In the faithful turtle-doue.

What if we new beauties see,
Will they not stir new affection?
I will thinke they pictures be,
(Image-like, of saints perfection)
Poorely counterfeting thee.

But your reasons purest light
Bids you leaue such minds to nourish.
Deere, do reason no such spite;
Neuer doth thy beauty florish
More then in my reasons sight.

But the wrongs Love beares will make
Love at length leaue undertaking.
No, the more fooles it doth shake,
In a ground of so firme making
Deeper still they driue the stake.

Peace, I thinke that some giue eare;
Come no more, least I get anger.
Blisse, I will my blisse forbeare;
Fearing, sweete, you to endanger;
But my soule shall harbour there.

Well, be gone; be gone, I say,
Lest that Argus eyes perceiue you.
O uniust is Fortunes sway,
Which can make me thus to leaue you,
And from lowts to run away.

CV

Unhappie sight, and hath shee vanisht by
　So nere, in so good time, so free a place!
Dead Glasse, dost thou thy obiect so imbrace,
　As what my hart still sees thou canst not spie!
I sweare by her I love and lacke, that I
　Was not in fault, who bent thy dazling race
Onely unto the heau'n of Stellas face,
　Counting but dust what in the way did lie.
But cease, mine eyes, your teares do witnesse well
　That you, guiltlesse thereof, your nectar mist:
Curst be the page from whome the bad torch fell:
　Curst be the night which did your strife resist:
　　Curst be the coachman that did driue so fast,
　　With no lesse curse then absence makes me tast.

CVI

O absent presence! Stella is not here;
  False-flatt'ring hope, that with so faire a face
Bare me in hand, that in this orphane place,
  Stella, I say my Stella, should appeare:
What saist thou now? where is that dainty cheere
  Thou toldst mine eyes should helpe their famisht case?
But thou art gone, now that selfe-felt disgrace
  Doth make me most to wish thy comfort neer.
But heere I do store of faire ladies meet,
  Who may with charme of conuersation sweete,
Make in my heauy mould new thoughts to grow.
  Sure they preuaile as much with me, as he
    That bad his friend, but then new maim'd to be
    Mery with him, and so forget his woe.

CVII

Stella, since thou so right a princesse art
  Of all the Powers which Life bestowes on me,
That ere by them ought undertaken be,
  They first resort unto that soueraigne part;
Sweete, for a while giue thy lieutenancie
  Which pants as though it still should leape to thee,
And on my thoughts give thy Lieftenancy
  To this great cause, which needes both use and art.
And as a Queene, who from her presence sends
  Whom she employes, dismisse from thee my wit,
Till it haue wrought what thy owne will attends.
  On seruants shame oft maisters blame doth sit:
    O let not fooles in me thy workes reproue,
    And scorning say, See what it is to love!

CVIII

When Sorrow (vsing mine owne fiers might)
   Melts downe his lead into my boyling brest
Through that darke furnace to my hart opprest,
   There shines a ioy from thee my only light:
But soone as thought of thee breeds my delight,
   And my yong soule flutters to thee his nest,
Most rude Despaire, my daily unbidden guest,
   Clips streight my wings, streight wraps me in his night,
And makes me then bow downe my heade, and say,
   Ah, what doth Phoebus gold that wretch auaile
Whom Iron doores doe keepe from vse of day?
   So strangely (alas) thy works on me preuaile,
     That in my woes for thee thou art my ioy,
     And in my ioyes for thee my onely annoy.

From *Certain Sonnets*

CIX

Thou blind mans marke, thou fooles selfe-chosen snare,
Fond fancies scum, and dregs of scatter'd thought:
Band of all euils, cradle of causelesse care;
   Thou web of will, whose end is neuer wrought:
   Desire! Desire! I haue too dearly bought,
With prise of mangled mind, thy worthlesse ware;
Too long, too long, asleepe thou hast me brought,
Who shouldst my mind to higher things prepare.
But yet in vaine thou hast my ruine sought;
   In vaine thou madest me to vaine things aspire;
   In vaine thou kindlest all thy smokie fire;
For Vertue hath this better lesson taught,--
   Within my selfe to seeke my onelie hire,
   Desiring nought but how to kill Desire.

CX

Leaue, me, O love which reachest but to dust,
And thou, my mind, aspire to higher things.
Grow rich in that which neuer taketh rust;
Whateuer fades, but fading pleasure brings.
  Draw in thy beames, and humble all thy might
To that sweet yoke where lasting freedomes be;
Which breakes the clowdes, and opens forth the light,
That doth both shine and giue us sight to see.
  O take fast hold; let that light be thy guide
In this small course which birth drawes out to death,
And thinke how euill becommeth him to slide,
Who seeketh heau'n, and comes of heau'nly breath.
  Then farewell world; thy vttermost I see:
  Eternall Love, maintaine thy life in me.
  Spendidis longum valedico nugis.

Delia

SAMUEL DANIEL

(1562-1619)

TO THE LADY MARY

COUNTESS OF PEMBROKE

Wonder of these, glory of other times,
O thou whom envy ev'n is forced t'admire!
Great Patroness of these my humble rhymes,
Which thou from out thy greatness dost inspire!
Since only thou has deigned to raise them higher,
Vouchsafe now to accept them as thine own,
Begotten by thy hand and my desire,
Wherein my zeal and thy great might is shown.
And seeing this unto the world is known,
O leave not still to grace thy work in me;
Let not the quickening seed be overthrown
Of that which may be born to honor thee,
   Whereof the travail I may challenge mine,
   But yet the glory, Madam, must be thine!

I

Unto the boundless ocean of thy beauty
Runs this poor river, charged with streams of zeal,
Returning thee the tribute of my duty,
Which here my love, my youth, my plaints reveal.
Here I unclasp the book of my charged soul,
Where I have cast th' accounts of all my care;
Here have I summed my sighs. Here I enrol
How they were spent for thee. Look, what they are.
Look on the dear expenses of my youth,
And see how just I reckon with thine eyes.
Examine well thy beauty with my truth,
And cross my cares ere greater sums arise.
   Read it, sweet maid, though it be done but slightly;
   Who can show all his love, doth love but lightly.

II

Go, wailing verse, the infants of my love,
Minerva-like, brought forth without a mother;
Present the image of the cares I prove,
Witness your father's grief exceeds all other.
Sigh out a story of her cruel deeds,
With interrupted accents of despair;
A monument that whosoever reads,
May justly praise and blame my loveless Fair;
Say her disdain hath dried up my blood,
And starved you, in succours still denying;
Press to her eyes, importune me some good,
Waken her sleeping pity with your crying:
    Knock at her hard heart, beg till you have moved
                            her,
    And tell th'unkind how dearly I have loved her.

III

If so it hap this offspring of my care,
These fatal anthems, lamentable songs,
Come to their view, who like afflicted are;
Let them yet sigh their own, and moan my wrongs.
But untouched hearts with unaffected eye,
Approach not to behold my soul's distress;
Clear-sighted you soon note what is awry,
Whilst blinded souls mine errors never guess.
You blinded souls, whom youth and error lead;
You outcast eaglets dazzled with your sun,
Do you, and none but you, my sorrows read;
You best can judge the wrongs that she hath done,
  That she hath done, the motive of my pain,
  Who whilst I love doth kill me with disdain.

IV

These plaintive verse, the posts of my desire,
Which haste for succour to her slow regard,
Bear not report of any slender fire,
Forging a grief to win a fame's reward.
Nor are my passions limned for outward hue,
For that no colours can depaint my sorrows;
Delia herself, and all the world may view
Best in my face where cares have tilled deep furrows.
No bays I seek to deck my mourning brow,
O clear-eyed rector of the holy hill!
My humble accents bear the olive bough
Of intercession but to move her will.
   These lines I use t'unburden mine own heart;
   My love affects no fame nor 'steems of art.

V

Whilst youth and error led my wandering mind,
And set my thoughts in heedless ways to range,
All unawares a goddess chaste I find,
Diana-like, to work my sudden change.
For her, no sooner had mine eye bewrayed,
But with disdain to see me in that place,
With fairest hand the sweet unkindest maid
Casts water-cold disdain upon my face.
Which turned my sport into a hart's despair,
Which still is chased, while I have any breath,
By mine own thoughts set on me by my Fair.
My thoughts like hounds pursue me to my death;
  Those that I fostered of mine own accord,
  Are made by her to murder thus their lord.

VI

Fair is my love, and cruel as she's fair;
Her brow shades frowns although her eyes are sunny;
Her smiles are lightning though her pride despair;
And her disdains are gall, her favours honey;
A modest maid, decked with a blush of honour,
Whose feet do tread green paths of youth and love;
The wonder of all eyes that look upon her,
Sacred on earth, designed a saint above.
Chastity and beauty, which were deadly foes,
Live reconciled friends within her brow;
And had she pity to conjoin with those,
Then who had heard the plaints I utter now?
  O had she not been fair and thus unkind,
  My Muse had slept and none had known my mind!

VII

For had she not been fair and thus unkind,
Then had no finger pointed at my lightness;
The world had never known what I do find,
And clouds obscure had shaded still her brightness.
Then had no censor's eye these lines surveyed,
Nor graver brows have judged my Muse so vain;
No sun my blush and error had bewrayed,
Nor yet the world had heard of such disdain.
Then had I walked with bold erected face;
No downcast look had signified my miss;
But my degraded hopes with such disgrace
Did force me groan out griefs and utter this.
  For being full, should I not then have spoken,
  My sense oppressed had failed and heart had
                        broken.

VIII

Thou, poor heart, sacrificed unto the fairest,
Hast sent the incense of thy sighs to heaven;
And still against her frowns fresh vows repairest,
And made thy passions with her beauty even.
And you, mine eyes, the agents of my heart,
Told the dumb message of my hidden grief;
And oft, with careful tunes, with silent art,
Did treat the cruel Fair to yield relief.
And you, my verse, the advocates of love,
Have followed hard the process of my case:
And urged that title which doth plainly prove
My faith should win, if justice might have place.
  Yet though I see that nought we do can move,
  'Tis not disdain must make me cease to love.

IX

If this be love, to draw a weary breath,
To paint on floods till the shore cry to th'air;
With downward looks still reading on the earth.
These sad memorials of my love's despair;
If this be love, to war against my soul,
Lie down to wail, rise up to sigh and grieve,
The never-resting stone of care to roll,
Still to complain my griefs, whilst none relieve;
If this be love, to clothe me with dark thoughts,
Haunting untrodden paths to wail apart,
My pleasures horror, music tragic notes,
Tears in mine eyes and sorrow at my heart;
 If this be love, to live a living death,
 Then do I love, and draw this weary breath.

X

Then do I love and draw this weary breath
For her, the cruel Fair, within whose brow
I written find the sentence of my death
In unkind letters wrote she cares not how.
Thou power that rul'st the confines of the night,
Laughter-loving goddess, worldly pleasures' queen,
Intenerate that heart that sets so light
The truest love that ever yet was seen;
And cause her leave to triumph in this wise
Upon the prostrate spoil of that poor heart
That serves, a trophy to her conquering eyes,
And must their glory to the world impart;
    Once let her know sh'hath done enough to prove
                                  me,
    And let her pity if she cannot love me!

XI

Tears, vows and prayers gain the hardest hearts,
Tears, vows and prayers have I spent in vain;
Tears cannot soften flint nor vows convert;
Prayers prevail not with a quaint disdain.
I lose my tears where I have lost my love,
I vow my faith where faith is not regarded,
I pray in vain a merciless to move;
So rare a faith ought better be rewarded.
Yet though I cannot win her will with tears,
Though my soul's idol scorneth all my vows,
Though all my prayers be to so deaf ears,
No favour though the cruel Fair allows,
   Yet will I weep, vow, pray to cruel she;
   Flint, frost, disdain, wears, melts and yields, we see.

XII

My spotless love hovers with purest wings
About the temple of the proudest frame,
Where blaze those lights, fairest of earthly things;
Which clear our clouded world with brightest flame.
M'ambitious thoughts, confined in her face,
Affect no honour but what she can give;
My hopes do rest in limits of her grace;
I weigh no comfort unless she relieve.
For she that can my heart imparadise,
Holds in her fairest hand what dearest is.
My fortune's wheel's the circle of her eyes,
Whose rolling grace deign once a turn of bliss.
  All my life's sweet consists in her alone,
  So much I love the most unloving one.

XIII

Behold what hap Pygmalion had to frame
And carve his proper grief upon a stone!
My heavy fortune is much like the same;
I work on flint and that's the cause I moan.
For hapless lo, even with mine own desires
I figured on the table of my heart
The fairest form that the world's eye admires,
And so did perish by my proper art.
And still I toil to change the marble breast
Of her whose sweetest grace I do adore,
Yet cannot find her breathe unto my rest.
Hard is her heart, and woe is me therefore.
    O happy he that joyed his stone and art!
    Unhappy I, to love a stony heart!

XIV

Those snary locks are those same nets, my dear,
Wherewith my liberty thou didst surprise
Love was the flame that fired me so near,
The dart transpiercing were those crystal eyes.
Strong is the net, and fervent is the flame;
Deep is the wound my sighs can well report.
Yet I do love, adore, and praise the same,
That holds, that burns, that wounds in this sort;
And list not seek to break, to quench, to heal,
The bond, the flame, the wound that festereth so,
By knife, by liquor, or by salve to deal;
So much I please to perish in my woe.
  Yet lest long travails be above my strength,
  Good Delia, loose, quench, heal me, now at length!

XV

If that a loyal heart and faith unfeigned,
If a sweet languish with a chaste desire,
If hunger-starven thoughts so long retained,
Fed but with smoke, and cherished but with fire;
And if a brow with care's characters painted
Bewray my love with broken words half spoken
To her which sits in my thoughts' temple sainted,
And lays to view my vulture-gnawn heart open;
If I have done due homage to her eyes,
And had my sighs still tending on her name,
If on her love my life and honour lies,
And she, th'unkindest maid, still scorns the same;
  Let this suffice, that all the world may see
  The fault is hers, though mine the hurt must be.

XVI

Happy in sleep, waking content to languish,
Embracing clouds by night, in daytime mourn,
My joys but shadows, touch of truth my anguish,
Griefs ever springing, comforts never born;
And still expecting when she will relent,
Grown hoarse with crying, "mercy, mercy give,'
So many vows and prayers having spent
That weary of my life I loathe to live;
And yet the hydra of my cares renews
Still new-born sorrows of her fresh disdain;
And still my hope the summer winds pursues,
Finding no end nor period of my pain;
    This is my state, my griefs do touch so nearly,
    And thus I live because I love her dearly.

XVII

Why should I sing in verse? Why should I frame
These sad neglected notes for her dear sake?
Why should I offer up unto her name,
The sweetest sacrifice my youth can make?
Why should I strive to make her live for ever,
That never deigns to give me joy to live?
Why should m'afflicted Muse so much endeavour
Such honour unto cruelty to give?
If her defects have purchased her this fame,
What should her virtues do, her smiles, her love?
If this her worst, how should her best inflame?
What passions would her milder favours move?
  Favours, I think, would sense quite overcome;
  And that makes happy lovers ever dumb.

XVIII

Since the first look that led me to this error,
To this thoughts' maze to my confusion tending,
Still have I lived in grief, in hope, in terror,
The circle of my sorrows never ending;
Yet cannot leave her love that holds me hateful;
Her eyes exact it, though her heart disdains me.
See what reward he hath that serves th'ungrateful?
So true and loyal love no favour gains me.
Still must I whet my young desires abated,
Upon the flint of such a heart rebelling;
And all in vain; her pride is so innated,
She yields no place at all for pity's dwelling.
   Oft have I told her that my soul did love her,
   And that with tears; yet all this will not move her.

XIX

Restore thy tresses to the golden ore,
Yield Cytherea's son those arks of love;
Bequeath the heavens the stars that I adore,
And to the orient do thy pearls remove;
Yield thy hands' pride unto the ivory white;
T'Arabian odours give thy breathing sweet;
Restore thy blush unto Aurora bright;
To Thetis give the honour of thy feet.
Let Venus have the graces she resigned,
And thy sweet voice give back unto the spheres;
But yet restore thy fierce and cruel mind
To Hyrcan tigers and to ruthless bears;
   Yield to the marble thy hard heart again;
   So shalt thou cease to plague, and I to pain.

XX

What it is to breathe and live without life;
How to be pale with anguish, red with fear,
T'have peace abroad, and nought within but strife:
Wish to be present, and yet shun t'appear;
How to be bold far off, and bashful near;
How to think much, and have no words to speak;
To crave redress, yet hold affliction dear;
To have affection strong, a body weak,
Never to find, yet evermore to seek;
And seek that which I dare not hope to find;
T'affect this life and yet this life disleek,
Grateful t'another, to myself unkind:
   This cruel knowledge of these contraries,
   Delia, my heart hath learned out of those eyes.

XXI

If beauty thus be clouded with a frown,
That pity shines no comfort to my bliss,
And vapours of disdain so overgrown,
That my life's light wholly indarkened is,
Why should I more molest the world with cries,
The air with sighs, the earth below with tears,
Since I live hateful to those ruthful eyes,
Vexing with untuned moan her dainty ears!
If I have loved her dearer than my breath,
My breath that calls the heaven to witness it!-
And still hold her most dear until my death,
And if that all this cannot move one whit,
   Yet sure she cannot but must think apart
   She doth me wrong to grieve so true a heart.

XXII

Come Time, the anchor hold of my desire,
My last resort whereto my hopes appeal;
Cause once the date of her disdain t'exspire,
Make her the sentence of her wrath repeal.
Rob her fair brow, break in on beauty, steal
Power from those eyes which pity cannot spare;
Deal with those dainty cheeks, as she doth deal
With this poor heart consumed with despair.
This heart made now the prospective of care
By loving her, the cruelst fair that lives,
The cruelst fair that sees I pine for her,
And never mercy to thy merit gives.
  Let her not still triumph over the prize
  Of mine affections taken by her eyes.

XXIII

Time, cruel Time, come and subdue that brow
Which conquers all but thee, and thee too stays,
As if she were exempt from scythe or bow,
From love or years unsubject to decays.
Or art thou grown in league with those fair eyes,
That they may help thee to consume our days?
Or dost thou spare her for her cruelties,
Being merciless like thee that no man weighs?
And yet thou seest thy power she disobeys,
Cares not for thee, but lets thee waste in vain,
And prodigal of hours and years betrays
Beauty and youth t'opinion and disdain.
  Yet spare her, Time; let her exempted be;
  She may become more kind to thee or me.

XXIV

These sorrowing sighs, the smoke of mine annoy,
These tears, which heat of sacred flame distils,
Are those due tributes that my faith doth pay
Unto the tyrant whose unkindness kills.
I sacrifice my youth and blooming years
At her proud feet, and she respects not it;
My flower, untimely's withered with my tears,
By winter woes for spring of youth unfit.
She thinks a look may recompense my care,
And so with looks prolongs my long-looked ease;
As short that bliss, so is the comfort rare;
Yet must that bliss my hungry thoughts appease.
  Thus she returns my hopes so fruitless ever;
  Once let her love indeed, or eye me never!

XXV

False hope prolongs my ever certain grief,
Traitor to me, and faithful to my love.
A thousand times it promised me relief,
Yet never any true effect I prove.
Oft when I find in her no truth at all,
I banish her, and blame her treachery;
Yet soon again I must her back recall,
As one that dies without her company.
Thus often, as I chase my hope from me,
Straightway she hastes her unto Delia's eyes;
Fed with some pleasing look, there shall she be,
And so sent back. And thus my fortune lies;
   Looks feed my hope, hope fosters me in vain;
   Hopes are unsure when certain is my pain.

XXVI

Look in my griefs, and blame me not to mourn,
From care to care that leads a life so bad;
Th'orphan of fortune, born to be her scorn,
Whose clouded brow doth make my days so sad.
Long are their nights whose cares do never sleep,
Loathsome their days who never sun yet joyed;
The impression of her eyes do pierce so deep,
That thus I live both day and night annoyed.
Yet since the sweetest root yields fruit so sour,
Her praise from my complaint I may not part;
I love th'effect, the cause being of this power;
I'll praise her face and blame her flinty heart,
   Whilst we both make the world admire at us,
   Her for disdain, and me for loving thus.

XXVII

Reignin my thoughts, fair hand, sweet eye, rare voice!
Possess me whole, my heart's triumvirate!
Yet heavy heart, to make so hard a choice
Of such as spoil thy poor afflicted state!
For whilst they strive which shall be lord of all,
All my poor life by them is trodden down;
They all erect their trophies on my fall,
And yield me nought that gives them their renown.
When back I look, I sigh my freedom past,
And wail the state wherein I present stand,
And see my fortune ever like to last,
Finding me reined with such a heavy hand.
  What can I do but yield? and yield I do;
  And serve all three, and yet they spoil me too!

XXVIII

Alluding to the sparrow pursued by a hawk, that flew into the bosom of Zenocrates

Whilst by thy eyes pursued, my poor heart flew
Into the sacred refuge of thy breast;
Thy rigour in that sanctuary slew
That which thy succ'ring mercy should have blest.
No privilege of faith could it protect,
Faith being with blood and five years witness signed,
Wherein no show gave cause of least suspect,
For well thou saw'st my love and how I pined.
Yet no mild comfort would thy brow reveal,
No lightning looks which falling hopes erect;
What boots to laws of succour to appeal?
Ladies and tyrants never laws respect.
   Then there I die from whence my life should come,
   And by that hand whom such deeds ill become.

XXIX

Still in the trace of one perplexed thought,
My ceaseless cares continually run on,
Seeking in vain what I have ever sought,
One in my love, and her hard heart still one.
I who did never joy in other sun,
And have no stars but those that must fulfil
The work of rigour, fatally begun
Upon this heart whom cruelty will kill,
Injurious Delia!-yet, I love thee still,
And will whilst I shall draw this breath of mine;
I'll tell the world that I deserved but ill,
And blame myself, t'excuse that heart of thine;
   See then who sins the greater of us twain,
   I in my love, or thou in thy disdain.

XXX

Oft do I marvel whether Delia's eyes
Are eyes, or else two radiant stars that shine;
For how could nature ever thus devise
Of earth, on earth, a substance so divine?
Stars, sure, they are, whose motions rule desires,
And calm and tempest follow their aspects;
Their sweet appearing still such power inspires,
That makes the world admire so strange effects.
Yet whether fixed or wandering stars are they,
Whose influence rules the orb of my poor heart;
Fixed, sure, they are, but wandering make me stray
In endless errors whence I cannot part.
   Stars, then, not eyes, move you with milder view
   Your sweet aspect on him that honours you!

XXXI

The star of my mishap imposed this pain
To spend the April of my years in grief;
Finding my fortune ever in the wane,
With still fresh cares, supplied with no relief.
Yet thee I blame not, though for thee 'tis done;
But these weak wings presuming to aspire,
Which now are melted by thine eyes' bright sun
That makes me fall from off my high desire;
And in my fall I cry for help with speed,
No pitying eye looks back upon my fears;
No succour find I now when most I need:
My heats must drown in th'ocean of my tears,
  Which still must bear the title of my wrong,
  Caused by those cruel beams that were so strong.

XXXII

And yet I cannot reprehend the flight,
Or blame th'attempt, presuming so to soar;
The mounting venture for a high delight
Did make the honour of the fall the more.
For who gets wealth, that puts not from the shore?
Danger hath honours, great designs their fame,
Glory doth follow, courage goes before;
And though th'event oft answers not the same,
Suffice that high attempts have never shame.
The mean observer whom base safety keeps,
Lives without honour, dies without a name,
And in eternal darkness ever sleeps.
  And therefore, Delia, 'tis to me no blot
  To have attempted though attained thee not.

XXXIII

Raising my hopes on hills of high desire,
Thinking to scale the heaven of her heart,
My slender means presumed too high a part,
Her thunder of disdain forced me retire,
And threw me down to pain in all this fire,
Where lo, I languish in so heavy smart
Because th'attempt was far above my art;
Her pride brooked not poor souls should come so nigh
                                        her.
Yet, I protest, my high desiring will
Was not to dispossess her of her right;
Her sovereignty should have remained still;
I only sought the bliss to have her sight.
  Her sight, contented thus to see me spill,
  Framed my desires fit for her eyes to kill.

XXXIV

Why dost thou, Delia, credit so thy glass,
Gazing thy beauty deigned thee by the skies,
And dost not rather look on him, alas!
Whose state best shows the force of murdering eyes?
The broken tops of lofty trees declare
The fury of a mercy-wanting storm;
And of what force thy wounding graces are
Upon myself, you best may find the form.
Then leave thy glass, and gaze thyself on me;
That mirror shows what power is in thy face;
To view your form too much may danger be,
Narcissus changed t'a flower in such a case.
  And you are changed, but not t'a hyacinth;
  I fear your eye hath turned your heart to flint.

XXXV

I once may see when years shall wreck my wrong,
And golden hairs shall change to silver wire,
And those bright rays that kindle all this fire,
Shall fail in force, their working not so strong,
Then beauty, now the burden of my song,
Whose glorious blaze the world doth so admire,
Must yield up all to tyrant Time's desire;
Then fade those flowers that decked her pride so long.
When if she grieve to gaze her in her glass,
Which then presents her whiter-withered hue,
Go you, my verse, go tell her what she was,
For what she was, she best shall find in you.
  Your fiery heat lets not her glory pass,
  But phoenix-like shall make her live anew.

XXXVI

Look, Delia, how w'esteem the half-blown rose,
The image of thy blush, and summer's honour,
Whilst yet her tender bud doth undisclose
That full of beauty time bestows upon her.
No sooner spreads her glory in the air,
But straight her wide-blown pomp comes to decline;
She then is scorned that late adorned the fair;
So fade the roses of those cheeks of thine.
No April can revive thy withered flowers,
Whose springing grace adorns thy glory now;
Swift speedy time, feathered with flying hours,
Dissolves the beauty of the fairest brow.
   Then do not thou such treasure waste in vain,
   But love now whilst thou mayst be loved again.

XXXVII

But love whilst that thou mayst be loved again,
Now whilst thy May hath filled thy lap with flowers,
Now whilst thy beauty bears without a stain,
Now use thy summer smiles, ere winter lowers.
And whilst thou spread'st unto the rising sun,
The fairest flower that ever saw the light,
Now joy thy time before thy sweet be done;
And, Delia, think thy morning must have night,
And that thy brightness sets at length to west,
When thou wilt close up that which now thou showest,
And think the same becomes thy fading best,
Which then shall most inveil and shadow most.
  Men do not weigh the stalk for that it was,
  When once they find her flower, her glory pass.

XXXVIII

When men shall find thy flower, thy glory pass,
And thou with careful brow sitting alone
Received hast this message from thy glass
That tells the truth, and says that all is gone;
Fresh shalt thou see in me the wounds thou mad'st,
Though spent thy flame, in me the heat remaining.
I that have loved thee thus before thou fad'st,
My faith shall wax when thou art in thy waning.
The world shall find this miracle in me,
That fire can burn when all the matter's spent;
Then what my faith hath been thyself shalt see,
And that thou wast unkind thou mayst repent.
   Thou mayst repent that thou hast scorned my tears,
   When winter snows upon thy sable hairs.

XXXIX

When winter snows upon thy sable hairs,
And frost of age hath nipped thy beauties near,
When dark shall seem thy day that never clears,
And all lies withered that was held so dear;
Then take this picture which I here present thee,
Limned with a pencil not all unworthy;
Here see the gifts that God and nature lent thee,
Here read thyself and what I suffered for thee.
This may remain thy lasting monument,
Which happily posterity may cherish;
These colours with thy fading are not spent,
These may remain when thou and I shall perish.
  If they remain, then thou shalt live thereby;
  They will remain, and so thou canst not die.

XL

Thou canst not die whilst any zeal abound
In feeling hearts than can conceive these lines;
Though thou a Laura hast no Petrarch found,
In base attire yet clearly beauty shines.
And I though born within a colder clime,
Do feel mine inward heat as great-I know it;
He never had more faith, although more rhyme;
I love as well though he could better show it.
But I may add one feather to thy fame,
To help her flight throughout the fairest isle;
And if my pen could more enlarge thy name,
Then shouldst thou live in an immortal style.
  For though that Laura better limned be,
  Suffice, thou shalt be loved as well as she!

XLI

Be not displeased that these my papers should
Bewray unto the world how fair thou art;
Or that my wits have showed the best they could
The chastest flame that ever warmed heart.
Think not, sweet Delia, this shall be thy shame,
My muse should sound thy praise with mournful
                            warble.
How many live, the glory of whose name
Shall rest in ice, while thine is graved in marble!
Thou mayst in after ages live esteemed,
Unburied in these lines, reserved in pureness;
These shall entomb those eyes, that have redeemed
Me from the vulgar, thee from all obscureness.
  Although my careful accents never moved thee,
  Yet count it no disgrace that I loved thee.

XLII

Delia, these eyes that so admireth thine,
Have seen those walls which proud ambition reared
To check the world, how they entombed have lain
Within themselves, and on them ploughs have eared;
Yet never found that barbarous hand attained
The spoil of fame deserved by virtuous men,
Whose glorious actions luckily had gained
Th'eternal annals of a happy pen.
And therefore grieve not if thy beauties die
Though time do spoil thee of the fairest veil
That ever yet covered mortality,
And must instar the needle and the rail.
   That grace which doth more than inwoman thee,
   Lives in my lines and must eternal be.

XLIII

Most fair and lovely maid, look from the shore,
See thy Leander striving in these waves,
Poor soul quite spent, whose force can do no more.
Now send forth hope, for now calm pity saves,
And waft him to thee with those lovely eyes,
A happy convoy to a holy land.
Now show thy power, and where thy virtue lies;
To save thine own, stretch out the fairest hand.
Stretch out the fairest hand, a pledge of peace,
That hand that darts so right and never misses;
I shall forget old wrongs, my griefs shall cease;
And that which gave me wounds, I'll give it kisses.
  Once let the ocean of my care find shore,
    That thou be pleased, and I may sigh no more.

XLIV

Read in my face a volume of despairs,
The wailing Iliads of my tragic woe;
Drawn with my blood, and painted with my cares,
Wrought by her hand that I have honoured so.
Who whilst I burn, she sings at my soul's wrack,
Looking aloft from turret of her pride;
There my soul's tyrant joys her in the sack
Of her own seat, whereof I made her guide.
There do these smokes that from affliction rise,
Serve as an incense to a cruel dame;
A sacrifice thrice-grateful to her eyes,
Because their power serves to exact the same.
  Thus ruins she to satisfy her will,
  The temple where her name was honoured still.

XLV

My Delia hath the waters of mine eyes,
The ready handmaids on her grace t'attend,
That never fail to ebb, but ever rise;
For to their flow she never grants an end.
The ocean never did attend more duly
Upon his sovereign's course, the night's pale queen,
Nor paid the impost of his waves more truly,
Than mine unto her cruelty hath been.
Yet nought the rock of that hard heart can move,
Where beat these tears with zeal, and fury drives;
And yet, I'd rather languish in her love,
Than I would joy the fairest she that lives.
   And if I find such pleasure to complain,
    What should I do then if I should obtain?

XLVI

How long shall I in mine affliction mourn,
A burden to myself, distressed in mind;
When shall my interdicted hopes return
From out despair wherein they live confined?
When shall her troubled brow charged with disdain
Reveal the treasure which her smiles impart?
When shall my faith the happiness attain,
To break the ice that hath congealed her heart?
Unto herself, herself my love doth summon,
(If love in her hath any power to move)
And let her tell me, as she is a woman,
Whether my faith hath not deserved her love?
  I know her heart cannot but judge with me,
  Although her eyes my adversaries be.

XLVII

Beauty, sweet love, is like the morning dew,
Whose short refresh upon the tender green
Cheers for a time but till the sun doth show,
And straight 'tis gone as it had never been.
Soon doth it fade that makes the fairest flourish,
Short is the glory of the blushing rose,
The hue which thou so carefully dost nourish,
Yet which at length thou must be forced to lose.
When thou, surcharged with burden of thy years,
Shalt bend thy wrinkles homeward to the earth,
And that in beauty's lease expired appears
The date of age, the kalends of our death,-
   But ah! no more, this must not be foretold,
   For women grieve to think they must be old.

XLVIII

I must not grieve my love, whose eyes would read
Lines of delight, whereon her youth might smile;
Flowers have a time before they come to seed,
And she is young, and now must sport the while.
Ah sport, sweet maid, in season of these years,
And learn to gather flowers before they wither.
And where the sweetest blossoms first appears,
Let love and youth conduct thy pleasures thither.
Lighten forth smiles to clear the clouded air,
And calm the tempest which my sighs do raise;
Pity and smiles do best become the fair,
Pity and smiles shall yield thee lasting praise.
  Make me to say, when all my griefs are gone,
  Happy the heart that sighed for such a one!

XLIX

At the Author's going into Italy

Ah whither, poor forsaken, wilt thou go,
To go from sorrow and thine own distress,
When every place presents like face of woe,
And no remove can make thy sorrows less!
Yet go, forsaken! Leave these woods, these plains,
Leave her and all, and all for her that leaves
Thee and thy love forlorn, and both disdains,
And of both wrongful deems and ill conceives.
Seek out some place, and see if any place
Can give the least release unto thy grief;
Convey thee from the thought of thy disgrace,
Steal from thyself and be thy cares' own thief.
   But yet what comforts shall I hereby gain?
   Bearing the wound, I needs must feel the pain.

L

This Sonnet was made at the Author's being in Italy

Drawn with th'attractive virtue of her eyes,
My touched heart turns it to that happy coast,
My joyful north, where all my fortune lies,
The level of my hopes desired most;
There where my Delia, fairer than the sun,
Decked with her youth whereon the world doth smile,
Joys in that honour which her eyes have won,
Th'eternal wonder of our happy isle.
Flourish, fair Albion, glory of the north!
Neptune's best darling, held between his arms;
Divided from the world as better worth,
Kept for himself, defended from all harms!
    Still let disarmed peace deck her and thee;
    And Muse-foe Mars abroad far fostered be!

LI

Care-charmer sleep, son of the sable night,
Brother to death, in silent darkness born,
Relieve my languish, and restore the light;
With dark forgetting of my care return,
And let the day be time enough to mourn
The shipwreck of my ill-adventured youth;
Let waking eyes suffice to wail their scorn,
Without the torment of the night's untruth.
Cease, dreams, the images of day-desires,
To model forth the passions of the morrow;
Never let rising sun approve you liars,
To add more grief to aggravate my sorrow;
    Still let me sleep, embracing clouds in vain,
    And never wake to feel the day's disdain.

LII

Let others sing of knights and paladins,
In aged accents and untimely words,
Paint shadows in imaginary lines
Which well the reach of their high wits records;
But I must sing of thee and those fair eyes
Authentic shall my verse in time to come,
When yet th'unborn shall say, Lo, where she lies,
Whose beauty made him speak that else was dumb!
These are the arks, the trophies I erect,
That fortify thy name against old age;
And these thy sacred virtues must protect
Against the dark and time's consuming rage.
  Though th'error of my youth in them appear,
  Suffice, they show I lived and loved thee, dear.

LIII

As to the Roman that would free his land,
His error was his honour and renown;
And more the fame of his mistaking hand
Than if he had the tyrant overthrown.
So Delia, hath mine error made me known,
And my deceived attempt deserved more fame,
Than if had the victory mine own,
And thy hard heart had yielded up the same.
And so likewise renowned is thy blame;
Thy cruelty, thy glory; O strange case,
That errors should be graced that merit shame,
And sin of frowns bring honour to the face.
  Yet happy Delia that thou wast unkind,
   Though happier far, if thou would'st change thy
                         mind.

LIV

Like as the lute delights or else dislikes
As is his art that plays upon the same,
So sounds my Muse according as she strikes
On my heart-strings high tuned unto her fame.
Her touch doth cause the warble of the sound,
Which here I yield in lamentable wise,
A wailing descant on the sweetest ground,
Whose due reports give honour to her eyes;
Else harsh my style, untunable my Muse;
Hoarse sounds the voice that praiseth not her name;
If any pleasing relish here I use,
Then judge the world her beauty gives the same.
   For no ground else could make the music such,
   Nor other hand could give so sweet a touch.

LV

None other fame mine unambitious Muse
Affected ever but t'eternise thee;
All other honours do my hopes refuse,
Which meaner prized and momentary be.
For God forbid I should my papers blot
With mercenary lines with servile pen,
Praising virtues in them that have them not,
Basely attending on the hopes of men.
No, no, my verse respects not Thames, nor theatres;
Nor seeks it to be known unto the great;
But Avon, poor in fame, and poor in waters,
Shall have my song, where Delia hath her seat.
  Avon shall be my Thames, and she my song;
  No other prouder brooks shall hear my wrong.

LVI

Unhappy pen, and ill-accepted lines
That intimate in vain my chaste desire,
My chaste desire, which from dark sorrow shines,
Enkindled by her eyes' celestial fire;
Celestial fire, and unrespecting powers
Which pity not the wounds made by their might,
Showed in these lines, the work of careful hours,
The sacrifice here offered to her sight.
But since she weighs them not, this rests for me:
I'll moan myself, and hide the wrong I have,
And so content me that her frowns should be
To m'infant style the cradle and the grave.
   What though my Muse no honour get thereby;
   Each bird sings to herself, and so will I.

LVII

Lo here the impost of a faith entire,
That love doth pay, and her disdain extorts;
Behold the message of a chaste desire
That tells the world how much my grief imports.
These tributary passions, beauty's due,
I send those eyes, the cabinets of love;
That cruelty herself might grieve to view
Th'affliction her unkind disdain doth move.
And how I live, cast down from off all mirth,
Pensive, alone, only but with despair;
My joys abortive perish in their birth,
My griefs long-lived and care succeeding care.
  This is my state, and Delia's heart is such;
  I say no more, I fear I said too much.

Idea

MICHAEL DRAYTON

(1563-1631)

TO THE READER OF THESE SONNETS

Into these loves who but for passion looks,
At this first sight here let him lay them by,
And seek elsewhere in turning other books,
Which better may his labour satisfy.
No far-fetched sigh shall ever wound my breast;
Love from mine eye a tear shall never wring;
Nor in 'Ah me's!' my whining sonnets drest,
A libertine fantasticly I sing.
My verse is the true image of my mind,
Ever in motion, still desiring change;
To choice of all variety inclined,
And in all humours sportively I range.
    My muse is rightly of the English strain,
    That cannot long one fashion entertain.

IDEA

I

Like an adventurous sea-farer am I,
Who hath some long and dang'rous voyage been,
And called to tell of his discovery,
How far he sailed, what countries he had seen,
Proceeding from the port whence he put forth,
Shows by his compass how his course he steered,
When east, when west, when south, and when by north,
As how the pole to every place was reared,
What capes he doubled, of what continent,
The gulfs and straits that strangely he had past,
Where most becalmed, where with foul weather spent,
And on what rocks in peril to be cast:
    Thus in my love, time calls me to relate
    My tedious travels and oft-varying fate.

II

My heart was slain, and none but you and I;
Who should I think the murder should commit?
Since but yourself there was no creature by
But only I, guiltless of murdering it.
It slew itself; the verdict on the view
Do quit the dead, and me not accessary.
Well, well, I fear it will be proved by you,
The evidence so great a proof doth carry.
But O see, see, we need inquire no further!
Upon your lips the scarlet drops are found,
And in your eye the boy that did the murder,
Your cheeks yet pale since first he gave the wound!
    By this I see, however things be past,
    Yet heaven will still have murder out at last.

III

Taking my pen, with words to cast my woe,
Duly to count the sum of all my cares,
I find my griefs innumerable grow,
The reck'nings rise to millions of despairs.
And thus dividing of my fatal hours,
The payments of my love I read and cross;
Subtracting, set my sweets unto my sours,
My joys' arrearage leads me to my loss.
And thus mine eyes a debtor to thine eye,
Which by extortion gaineth all their looks,
My heart hath paid such grievous usury,
That all their wealth lies in thy beauty's books.
    And all is thine which hath been due to me,
    And I a bankrupt, quite undone by thee.

IV

Bright star of beauty, on whose eyelids sit
A thousand nymph-like and enamoured graces,
The goddesses of memory and wit,
Which there in order take their several places;
In whose dear bosom, sweet delicious love
Lays down his quiver which he once did bear,
Since he that blessèd paradise did prove,
And leaves his mother's lap to sport him there
Let others strive to entertain with words
My soul is of a braver mettle made;
I hold that vile which vulgar wit affords;
In me's that faith which time cannot invade.
    Let what I praise be still made good by you;
    Be you most worthy whilst I am most true!

V

Nothing but 'No!' and 'I!' and 'I!' and 'No!'
'How falls it out so strangely?' you reply.
I tell ye, Fair, I'll not be answered so,
With this affirming 'No!' denying 'I!'
I say 'I love!' You slightly answer 'I!'
I say 'You love!' You pule me out a 'No!'
I say 'I die!' You echo me with 'I!'
'Save me!' I cry; you sigh me out a 'No!'
Must woe and I have naught but 'No!' and 'I!'?
No 'I!' am I, if I no more can have.
Answer no more; with silence make reply,
And let me take myself what I do crave;
    Let 'No!' and 'I!' with I and you be so,
    Then answer 'No!' and 'I!' and 'I!' and 'No!'

VI

How many paltry, foolish, painted things,
That now in coaches trouble every street,
Shall be forgotten, whom no poet sings,
Ere they be well wrapped in their winding sheet!
Where I to thee eternity shall give,
When nothing else remaineth of these days,
And queens hereafter shall be glad to live
Upon the alms of thy superfluous praise;
Virgins and matrons reading these my rhymes,
Shall be so much delighted with thy story,
That they shall grieve they lived not in these times,
To have seen thee, their sex's only glory.
    So shalt thou fly above the vulgar throng,
    Still to survive in my immortal song.

VII

Love, in a humour, played the prodigal,
And bade my senses to a solemn feast;
Yet more to grace the company withal,
Invites my heart to be the chiefest guest.
No other drink would serve this glutton's turn,
But precious tears distilling from mine eyne,
Which with my sighs this epicure doth burn,
Quaffing carouses in this costly wine;
Where, in his cups, o'ercome with foul excess,
Straightways he plays a swaggering ruffian's part,
And at the banquet in his drunkenness,
Slew his dear friend, my kind and truest heart.
    A gentle warning, friends, thus may you see,
    What 'tis to keep a drunkard company!

VIII

There's nothing grieves me but that age should haste,
That in my days I may not see thee old;
That where those two clear sparkling eyes are placed,
Only two loopholes that I might behold;
That lovely archèd ivory-polished brow
Defaced with wrinkles, that I might but see;
Thy dainty hair, so curled and crispèd now,
Like grizzled moss upon some agèd tree;
Thy cheek now flush with roses, sunk and lean;
Thy lips, with age as any wafer thin!
Thy pearly teeth out of thy head so clean,
That when thou feed'st thy nose shall touch thy chin!
    These lines that now thou scornst, which should delight
                              thee,
    Then would I make thee read but to despite thee.

IX

As other men, so I myself do muse
Why in this sort I wrest invention so,
And why these giddy metaphors I use,
Leaving the path the greater part do go.
I will resolve you. I'm a lunatic;
And ever this in madmen you shall find,
What they last thought of when the brain grew sick,
In most distraction they keep that in mind.
Thus talking idly in this bedlam fit,
Reason and I, you must conceive, are twain;
'Tis nine years now since first I lost my wit.
Bear with me then though troubled be my brain.
    With diet and correction men distraught,
     Not too far past, may to their wits be brought.

X

To nothing fitter can I thee compare
Than to the son of some rich penny-father,
Who having now brought on his end with care,
Leaves to his son all he had heaped together.
This new rich novice, lavish of his chest,
To one man gives, doth on another spend;
Then here he riots; yet amongst the rest,
Haps to lend some to one true honest friend.
Thy gifts thou in obscurity dost waste:
False friends, thy kindness born but to deceive thee;
Thy love that is on the unworthy placed;
Time hath thy beauty which with age will leave thee.
    Only that little which to me was lent,
    I give thee back when all the rest is spent.

XI

You're not alone when you are still alone;
O God! from you that I could private be!
Since you one were, I never since was one;
Since you in me, myself since out of me.
Transported from myself into your being,
Though either distant, present yet to either;
Senseless with too much joy, each other seeing;
And only absent when we are together.
Give me my self, and take your self again!
Devise some means but how I may forsake you!
So much is mine that doth with you remain,
That taking what is mine, with me I take you.
    You do bewitch me! O that I could fly
    From my self you, or from your own self I!

TO THE SOUL

XII

That learned Father which so firmly proves
The soul of man immortal and divine,
And doth the several offices define
Anima. Gives her that name, as she the body moves.
Amor. Then is she love, embracing charity.
Animus. Moving a will in us, it is the mind;
Mens. Retaining knowledge, still the same in kind.
Memoria. As intellectual, it is memory.
Ratio. In judging, reason only is her name.
Sensus. In speedy apprehension, it is sense.
Conscientia. In right and wrong they call her conscience;
Spiritus. The spirit, when it to God-ward doth inflame:
    These of the soul the several functions be,
    Which my heart lightened by thy love doth see.

TO THE SHADOW

XIII

Letters and lines we see are soon defaced
Metals do waste and fret with canker's rust,
The diamond shall once consume to dust,
And freshest colours with foul stains disgraced;
Paper and ink can paint but naked words,
To write with blood of force offends the sight;
And if with tears, I find them all too light,
And sighs and signs a silly hope affords.
O sweetest shadow, how thou serv'st my turn!
Which still shalt be as long as there is sun,
Nor whilst the world is never shall be done;
Whilst moon shall shine or any fire shall burn,
    That everything whence shadow doth proceed,
    May in his shadow my love's story read.

HIS REMEDY FOR LOVE

XV

Since to obtain thee nothing me will stead,
I have a med'cine that shall cure my love.
The powder of her heart dried, when she's dead,
That gold nor honour ne'er had power to move;
Mixed with her tears that ne'er her true love crost,
Nor at fifteen ne'er longed to be a bride;
Boiled with her sighs, in giving up the ghost,
That for her late deceasèd husband died;
Into the same then let a woman breathe,
That being chid did never word reply;
With one thrice married's prayers, that did bequeath
A legacy to stale virginity.
    If this receipt have not the power to win me,
    Little I'll say, but think the devil's in me!

AN ALLUSION TO THE PHŒNIX

XVI

'Mongst all the creatures in this spacious round
Of the birds' kind, the phœnix is alone,
Which best by you of living things is known;
None like to that, none like to you is found!
Your beauty is the hot and splend'rous sun;
The precious spices be your chaste desire,
Which being kindled by that heavenly fire,
Your life, so like the phœnix's begun.
Yourself thus burnèd in that sacred flame,
With so rare sweetness all the heavens perfuming;
Again increasing as you are consuming,
Only by dying born the very same.
    And winged by fame you to the stars ascend;
    So you of time shall live beyond the end.

TO TIME

XVII

Stay, speedy time! Behold, before thou pass
From age to age, what thou hast sought to see,
One in whom all the excellencies be,
In whom heaven looks itself as in a glass.
Time, look thou too in this translucent glass,
And thy youth past in this pure mirror see!
As the world's beauty in his infancy,
What it was then, and thou before it was.
Pass on and to posterity tell this—
Yet see thou tell but truly what hath been.
Say to our nephews that thou once hast seen
In perfect human shape all heavenly bliss;
    And bid them mourn, nay more, despair with thee,
    That she is gone, her like again to see.

TO THE CELESTIAL NUMBERS

XVIII

To this our world, to learning, and to heaven,
Three nines there are, to every one a nine;
One number of the earth, the other both divine;
One woman now makes three odd numbers even.
Nine orders first of angels be in heaven;
Nine muses do with learning still frequent:
These with the gods are ever resident.
Nine worthy women to the world were given.
My worthy one to these nine worthies addeth;
And my fair Muse, one Muse unto the nine.
And my good angel, in my soul divine!—
With one more order these nine orders gladdeth.
    My Muse, my worthy, and my angel then
    Makes every one of these three nines a ten.

TO HUMOUR

XIX

You cannot love, my pretty heart, and why?
There was a time you told me that you would,
But how again you will the same deny.
If it might please you, would to God you could!
What, will you hate? Nay, that you will not neither;
Nor love, nor hate! How then? What will you do?
What, will you keep a mean then betwixt either?
Or will you love me, and yet hate me too?
Yet serves not this! What next, what other shift?
You will, and will not; what a coil is here!
I see your craft, now I perceive your drift,
And all this while I was mistaken there.
    Your love and hate is this, I now do prove you:
    You love in hate, by hate to make me love you.

XX

An evil spirit, your beauty, haunts me still,
Wherewith, alas, I have been long possessed!
Which ceaseth not to tempt me to each ill,
Nor give me once but one poor minute's rest.
In me it speaks whether I sleep or wake;
And when by means to drive it out I try,
With greater torments then it me doth take,
And tortures me in most extremity.
Before my face it lays down my despairs,
And hastes me on unto a sudden death;
Now tempting me to drown myself in tears,
And then in sighing to give up my breath.
 Thus am I still provoked to every evil,
 By this good wicked spirit, sweet angel-devil.

XXI

A witless gallant a young wench that wooed—
Yet his dull spirit her not one jot could move—
Intreated me as e'er I wished his good,
To write him but one sonnet to his love.
When I as fast as e'er my pen could trot,
Poured out what first from quick invention came,
Nor never stood one word thereof to blot;
Much like his wit that was to use the same.
But with my verses he his mistress won,
Who doated on the dolt beyond all measure.
But see, for you to heaven for phrase I run,
And ransack all Apollo's golden treasure!
    Yet by my troth, this fool his love obtains,
    And I lose you for all my wit and pains!

TO FOLLY

XXII

With fools and children good discretion bears;
Then, honest people, bear with love and me,
Nor older yet nor wiser made by years,
Amongst the rest of fools and children be.
Love, still a baby, plays with gauds and toys,
And like a wanton sports with every feather,
And idiots still are running after boys;
Then fools and children fitt'st to go together.
He still as young as when he first was born,
Nor wiser I than when as young as he;
You that behold us, laugh us not to scorn;
Give nature thanks you are not such as we!
    Yet fools and children sometimes tell in play;
    Some wise in show, more fools indeed than they.

XXIII

Love, banished heaven, in earth was held in scorn,
Wand'ring abroad in need and beggary;
And wanting friends, though of a goddess born,
Yet craved the alms of such as passèd by.
I, like a man devout and charitable,
Clothèd the naked, lodged this wandering guest;
With sighs and tears still furnishing his table
With what might make the miserable blest.
But this ungrateful for my good desert,
Enticed my thoughts against me to conspire,
Who gave consent to steal away my heart,
And set my breast, his lodging, on a fire.
    Well, well, my friends, when beggars grow thus bold,
    No marvel then though charity grow cold.

XXIV

I hear some say, 'This man is not in love!'
'Who! can he love? a likely thing!' they say.
'Read but his verse, and it will easily prove!'
O, judge not rashly, gentle Sir, I pray!
Because I loosely trifle in this sort,
As one that fain his sorrows would beguile,
You now suppose me all this time in sport,
And please yourself with this conceit the while.
Ye shallow cens'rers! sometimes, see ye not,
In greatest perils some men pleasant be,
Where fame by death is only to be got,
They resolute! So stands the case with me.
    Where other men in depth of passion cry,
    I laugh at fortune, as in jest to die.

XXV

O, why should nature niggardly restrain
That foreign nations relish not our tongue?
Else should my lines glide on the waves of Rhine,
And crown the Pyren's with my living song.
But bounded thus, to Scotland get you forth!
Thence take you wing unto the Orcades!
There let my verse get glory in the north,
Making my sighs to thaw the frozen seas.
And let the bards within that Irish isle,
To whom my Muse with fiery wings shall pass,
Call back the stiff-necked rebels from exile,
And mollify the slaughtering gallowglass;
    And when my flowing numbers they rehearse,
    Let wolves and bears be charmèd with my verse.

TO DESPAIR

XXVI

I ever love where never hope appears,
Yet hope draws on my never-hoping care,
And my life's hope would die but for despair;
My never certain joy breeds ever certain fears.
Uncertain dread gives wings unto my hope;
Yet my hope's wings are laden so with fear
As they cannot ascend to my hope's sphere,
Though fear gives them more than a heavenly scope.
Yet this large room is bounded with despair,
So my love is still fettered with vain hope,
And liberty deprives him of his scope,
And thus am I imprisoned in the air.
    Then, sweet despair, awhile hold up thy head,
    Or all my hope for sorrow will be dead.

XXVII

Is not love here as 'tis in other climes,
And differeth it as do the several nations?
Or hath it lost the virtue with the times,
Or in this island alt'reth with the fashions?
Or have our passions lesser power than theirs,
Who had less art them lively to express?
Is nature grown less powerful in their heirs,
Or in our fathers did she more transgress?
I am sure my sighs come from a heart as true
As any man's that memory can boast,
And my respects and services to you,
Equal with his that loves his mistress most.
    Or nature must be partial in my cause,
    Or only you do violate her laws.

XXVIII

To such as say thy love I overprize,
And do not stick to term my praises folly,
Against these folks that think themselves so wise,
I thus oppose my reason's forces wholly:
Though I give more than well affords my state,
In which expense the most suppose me vain
Which yields them nothing at the easiest rate,
Yet at this price returns me treble gain;
They value not, unskilful how to use,
And I give much because I gain thereby.
I that thus take or they that thus refuse,
Whether are these deceivèd then, or I?
    In everything I hold this maxim still,
    The circumstance doth make it good or ill.

TO THE SENSES

XXIX

When conquering love did first my heart assail,
Unto mine aid I summoned every sense,
Doubting if that proud tyrant should prevail,
My heart should suffer for mine eyes' offence.
But he with beauty first corrupted sight,
My hearing bribed with her tongue's harmony,
My taste by her sweet lips drawn with delight,
My smelling won with her breath's spicery,
But when my touching came to play his part,
The king of senses, greater than the rest,
He yields love up the keys unto my heart,
And tells the others how they should be blest.
    And thus by those of whom I hoped for aid,
    To cruel love my soul was first betrayed.

TO THE VESTALS

XXX

Those priests which first the vestal fire begun,
Which might be borrowed from no earthly flame,
Devised a vessel to receive the sun,
Being stedfastly opposèd to the same;
Where with sweet wood laid curiously by art,
On which the sun might by reflection beat,
Receiving strength for every secret part,
The fuel kindled with celestial heat.
Thy blessèd eyes, the sun which lights this fire,
My holy thoughts, they be the vestal flame,
Thy precious odours be my chaste desires,
My breast's the vessel which includes the same;
    Thou art my Vesta, thou my goddess art,
    Thy hallowed temple only is my heart.

TO THE CRITICS

XXXI

Methinks I see some crooked mimic jeer,
And tax my Muse with this fantastic grace;
Turning my papers asks, 'What have we here?'
Making withal some filthy antic face.
I fear no censure nor what thou canst say,
Nor shall my spirit one jot of vigour lose.
Think'st thou, my wit shall keep the packhorse way,
That every dudgeon low invention goes?
Since sonnets thus in bundles are imprest,
And every drudge doth dull our satiate ear,
Think'st thou my love shall in those rags be drest
That every dowdy, every trull doth wear?
    Up to my pitch no common judgment flies;
    I scorn all earthly dung-bred scarabies.

TO THE RIVER ANKOR

XXXII

Our floods' queen, Thames, for ships and swans is
crowned,
And stately Severn for her shore is praised;
The crystal Trent for fords and fish renowned,
And Avon's fame to Albion's cliff is raised.
Carlegion Chester vaunts her holy Dee;
York many wonders of her Ouse can tell;
The Peak, her Dove, whose banks so fertile be;
And Kent will say her Medway doth excel.
Cotswold commends her Isis to the Thame;
Our northern borders boast of Tweed's fair flood;
Our western parts extol their Wilis' fame;
And the old Lea brags of the Danish blood.
    Arden's sweet Ankor, let thy glory be,
    That fair Idea only lives by thee!

TO IMAGINATION

XXXIII

Whilst yet mine eyes do surfeit with delight,
My woful heart imprisoned in my breast,
Wisheth to be transformèd to my sight,
That it like those by looking might be blest.
But whilst mine eyes thus greedily do gaze,
Finding their objects over-soon depart,
These now the other's happiness do praise,
Wishing themselves that they had been my heart,
That eyes were heart, or that the heart were eyes,
As covetous the other's use to have.
But finding nature their request denies,
This to each other mutually they crave;
    That since the one cannot the other be,
    That eyes could think of that my heart could see.

TO ADMIRATION

XXXIV

Marvel not, love, though I thy power admire,
Ravished a world beyond the farthest thought,
And knowing more than ever hath been taught,
That I am only starved in my desire.
Marvel not, love, though I thy power admire,
Aiming at things exceeding all perfection,
To wisdom's self to minister direction,
That I am only starved in my desire.
Marvel not, love, though I thy power admire,
Though my conceit I further seem to bend
Than possibly invention can extend,
And yet am only starved in my desire.
    If thou wilt wonder, here's the wonder, love,
    That this to me doth yet no wonder prove.

TO MIRACLE

XXXV

Some misbelieving and profane in love,
When I do speak of miracles by thee,
May say that thou art flatterèd by me,
Who only write my skill in verse to prove
See miracles, ye unbelieving, see!
A dumb-born Muse made to express the mind,
A cripple hand to write, yet lame by kind,
One by thy name, the other touching thee.
Blind were mine eyes, till they were seen of thine;
And mine ears deaf by thy fame healèd be;
My vices cured by virtues sprung from thee;
My hopes revived which long in grave had lien.
    All unclean thoughts, foul spirits, cast out in me,
    Only by virtue that proceeds from thee.

CUPID CONJURED

XXXVI

Thou purblind boy, since thou hast been so slack
To wound her heart whose eyes have wounded me
And suffered her to glory in my wrack,
Thus to my aid I lastly conjure thee!
By hellish Styx, by which the Thund'rer swears,
By thy fair mother's unavoided power,
By Hecate's names, by Proserpine's sad tears,
When she was wrapt to the infernal bower!
By thine own lovèd Psyche, by the fires
Spent on thine altars flaming up to heaven,
By all true lovers' sighs, vows, and desires,
By all the wounds that ever thou hast given;
    I conjure thee by all that I have named,
    To make her love, or, Cupid, be thou damned!

XXXVII

Dear, why should you command me to my rest,
When now the night doth summon all to sleep?
Methinks this time becometh lovers best;
Night was ordained together friends to keep.
How happy are all other living things,
Which though the day disjoin by several flight,
The quiet evening yet together brings,
And each returns unto his love at night!
O thou that art so courteous else to all,
Why shouldst thou, Night, abuse me only thus,
That every creature to his kind dost call,
And yet 'tis thou dost only sever us?
    Well could I wish it would be ever day,
    If when night comes, you bid me go away.

XXXVIII

Sitting alone, love bids me go and write;
Reason plucks back, commanding me to stay,
Boasting that she doth still direct the way,
Or else love were unable to indite.
Love growing angry, vexèd at the spleen,
And scorning reason's maimèd argument,
Straight taxeth reason, wanting to invent
Where she with love conversing hath not been.
Reason reproachèd with this coy disdain,
Despiteth love, and laugheth at her folly;
And love contemning reason's reason wholly,
Thought it in weight too light by many a grain.
    Reason put back doth out of sight remove,
    And love alone picks reason out of love.

XXXIX

Some, when in rhyme they of their loves do tell,
With flames and lightnings their exordiums paint.
Some call on heaven, some invocate on hell,
And Fates and Furies, with their woes acquaint.
Elizium is too high a seat for me,
I will not come in Styx or Phlegethon,
The thrice-three Muses but too wanton be,
Like they that lust, I care not, I will none.
Spiteful Erinnys frights me with her looks,
My manhood dares not with foul Ate mell,
I quake to look on Hecate's charming books,
I still fear bugbears in Apollo's cell.
  I pass not for Minerva, nor Astrea,
  Only I call on my divine Idea!

XL

My heart the anvil where my thoughts do beat,
My words the hammers fashioning my desire,
My breast the forge including all the heat,
Love is the fuel which maintains the fire;
My sighs the bellows which the flame increaseth,
Filling mine ears with noise and nightly groaning;
Toiling with pain, my labour never ceaseth,
In grievous passions my woes still bemoaning;
My eyes with tears against the fire striving,
Whose scorching gleed my heart to cinders turneth;
But with those drops the flame again reviving,
Still more and more it to my torment burneth,
    With Sisyphus thus do I roll the stone,
    And turn the wheel with damnèd Ixion.

LOVE'S LUNACY

XLI

Why do I speak of joy or write of love,
When my heart is the very den of horror,
And in my soul the pains of hell I prove,
With all his torments and infernal terror?
What should I say? what yet remains to do?
My brain is dry with weeping all too long;
My sighs be spent in utt'ring of my woe,
And I want words wherewith to tell my wrong.
But still distracted in love's lunacy,
And bedlam-like thus raving in my grief,
Now rail upon her hair, then on her eye,
Now call her goddess, then I call her thief;
    Now I deny her, then I do confess her,
    Now do I curse her, then again I bless her.

XLII

Some men there be which like my method well,
And much commend the strangeness of my vein;
Some say I have a passing pleasing strain,
Some say that in my humour I excel.
Some who not kindly relish my conceit,
They say, as poets do, I use to feign,
And in bare words paint out by passions' pain.
Thus sundry men their sundry minds repeat.
I pass not, I, how men affected be,
Nor who commends or discommends my verse!
It pleaseth me if I my woes rehearse,
And in my lines if she my love may see.
    Only my comfort still consists in this,
    Writing her praise I cannot write amiss.

XLIII

Why should your fair eyes with such sov'reign grace
Disperse their rays on every vulgar spirit,
Whilst I in darkness in the self-same place,
Get not one glance to recompense my merit?
So doth the plowman gaze the wand'ring star,
And only rest contented with the light,
That never learned what constellations are,
Beyond the bent of his unknowing sight.
O why should beauty, custom to obey,
To their gross sense apply herself so ill!
Would God I were as ignorant as they,
When I am made unhappy by my skill,
  Only compelled on this poor good to boast!
  Heavens are not kind to them that know them most.

XLIV

Whilst thus my pen strives to eternise thee,
Age rules my lines with wrinkles in my face,
Where in the map of all my misery
Is modelled out the world of my disgrace;
Whilst in despite of tyrannising times,
Medea-like, I make thee young again,
Proudly thou scorn'st my world-outwearing rhymes,
And murther'st virtue with thy coy disdain;
And though in youth my youth untimely perish,
To keep thee from oblivion and the grave,
Ensuing ages yet my rhymes shall cherish,
Where I intombed my better part shall save;
    And though this earthly body fade and die,
    My name shall mount upon eternity.

XLV

Muses which sadly sit about my chair,
Drowned in the tears extorted by my lines;
With heavy sighs whilst thus I break the air,
Painting my passions in these sad designs,
Since she disdains to bless my happy verse,
The strong built trophies to her living fame,
Ever henceforth my bosom be your hearse,
Wherein the world shall now entomb her name.
Enclose my music, you poor senseless walls,
Sith she is deaf and will not hear my moans;
Soften yourselves with every tear that falls,
Whilst I like Orpheus sing to trees and stones,
    Which with my plaint seem yet with pity moved,
    Kinder than she whom I so long have loved.

XLVI

Plain-pathed experience, the unlearnèd's guide,
Her simple followers evidently shows
Sometimes what schoolmen scarcely can decide,
Nor yet wise reason absolutely knows;
In making trial of a murder wrought,
If the vile actors of the heinous deed
Near the dead body happily be brought,
Oft 't hath been proved the breathless corse will bleed.
She coming near, that my poor heart hath slain,
Long since departed, to the world no more,
The ancient wounds no longer can contain,
But fall to bleeding as they did before.
    But what of this? Should she to death be led,
    It furthers justice but helps not the dead.

XLVII

In pride of wit, when high desire of fame
Gave life and courage to my lab'ring pen,
And first the sound and virtue of my name
Won grace and credit in the ears of men,
With those the throngèd theatres that press,
I in the circuit for the laurel strove,
Where the full praise I freely must confess,
In heat of blood a modest mind might move;
With shouts and claps at every little pause,
When the proud round on every side hath rung,
Sadly I sit unmoved with the applause,
As though to me it nothing did belong.
    No public glory vainly I pursue;
    All that I seek is to eternise you.

XLVIII

Cupid, I hate thee, which I'd have thee know;
A naked starveling ever mayst thou be!
Poor rogue, go pawn thy fascia and thy bow
For some poor rags wherewith to cover thee;
Or if thou'lt not thy archery forbear,
To some base rustic do thyself prefer,
And when corn's sown or grown into the ear,
Practice thy quiver and turn crowkeeper;
Or being blind, as fittest for the trade,
Go hire thyself some bungling harper's boy;
They that are blind are minstrels often made,
So mayst thou live to thy fair mother's joy;
    That whilst with Mars she holdeth her old way,
    Thou, her blind son, mayst sit by them and play.

XLIX

Thou leaden brain, which censur'st what I write,
And sayst my lines be dull and do not move,
I marvel not thou feel'st not my delight,
Which never felt'st my fiery touch of love;
But thou whose pen hath like a packhorse served,
Whose stomach unto gall hath turned thy food,
Whose senses like poor prisoners, hunger-starved
Whose grief hath parched thy body, dried thy blood;
Thou which hast scornèd life and hated death,
And in a moment, mad, sober, glad, and sorry;
Thou which hast banned thy thoughts and curst thy birth
With thousand plagues more than in purgatory;
    Thou thus whose spirit love in his fire refines,
    Come thou and read, admire, applaud my lines!

L

As in some countries far remote from hence,
The wretched creature destinèd to die,
Having the judgment due to his offence,
By surgeons begged, their art on him to try,
Which on the living work without remorse,
First make incision on each mastering vein,
Then staunch the bleeding, then transpierce the corse,
And with their balms recure the wounds again,
Then poison and with physic him restore;
Not that they fear the hopeless man to kill,
But their experience to increase the more:
Even so my mistress works upon my ill,
    By curing me and killing me each hour,
    Only to show her beauty's sovereign power.

LI

Calling to mind since first my love begun,
Th'uncertain times, oft varying in their course,
How things still unexpectedly have run,
As't please the Fates by their resistless force;
Lastly, mine eyes amazedly have seen
Essex's great fall, Tyrone his peace to gain,
The quiet end of that long living Queen,
This King's fair entrance, and our peace with Spain,
We and the Dutch at length ourselves to sever;
Thus the world doth and evermore shall reel;
Yet to my goddess am I constant ever,
Howe'er blind Fortune turn her giddy wheel;
     Though heaven and earth prove both to me untrue,
     Yet am I still inviolate to you.

LII

What dost thou mean to cheat me of my heart,
To take all mine and give me none again?
Or have thine eyes such magic or that art
That what they get they ever do retain?
Play not the tyrant but take some remorse;
Rebate thy spleen if but for pity's sake;
Or cruel, if thou can'st not, let us scorse,
And for one piece of thine my whole heart take.
But what of pity do I speak to thee,
Whose breast is proof against complaint or prayer?
Or can I think what my reward shall be
From that proud beauty which was my betrayer!
    What talk I of a heart when thou hast none?
    Or if thou hast, it is a flinty one.

ANOTHER TO THE RIVER ANKOR

LIII

Clear Ankor, on whose silver-sanded shore,
My soul-shrined saint, my fair Idea lives;
O blessèd brook, whose milk-white swans adore
Thy crystal stream, refinèd by her eyes,
Where sweet myrrh-breathing Zephyr in the spring
Gently distils his nectar-dropping showers,
Where nightingales in Arden sit and sing
Amongst the dainty dew-impearlèd flowers;
Say thus, fair brook, when thou shalt see thy queen,
'Lo, here thy shepherd spent his wand'ring years
And in these shades, dear nymph, he oft hath been;
And here to thee he sacrificed his tears.'
    Fair Arden, thou my Tempe art alone,
    And thou, sweet Ankor, art my Helicon!

LIV

Yet read at last the story of my woe,
The dreary abstracts of my endless cares,
With my life's sorrow interlinèd so,
Smoked with my sighs, and blotted with my tears,
The sad memorials of my miseries,
Penned in the grief of mine afflicted ghost,
My life's complaint in doleful elegies,
With so pure love as time could never boast.
Receive the incense which I offer here,
By my strong faith ascending to thy fame,
My zeal, my hope, my vows, my praise, my prayer,
My soul's oblations to thy sacred name;
  Which name my Muse to highest heavens shall raise,
  By chaste desire, true love, and virtuous praise.

LV

My fair, if thou wilt register my love,
A world of volumes shall thereof arise;
Preserve my tears, and thou thyself shall prove
A second flood down raining from mine eyes;
Note but my sighs, and thine eyes shall behold
The sunbeams smothered with immortal smoke;
And if by thee my prayers may be enrolled,
They heaven and earth to pity shall provoke.
Look thou into my breast, and thou shalt see
Chaste holy vows for my soul's sacrifice,
That soul, sweet maid, which so hath honoured thee,
Erecting trophies to thy sacred eyes,
    Those eyes to my heart shining ever bright,
    When darkness hath obscured each other light.

AN ALLUSION TO THE EAGLETS

LVI

When like an eaglet I first found my love,
For that the virtue I thereof would know,
Upon the nest I set it forth to prove
If it were of that kingly kind or no;
But it no sooner saw my sun appear,
But on her rays with open eyes it stood,
To show that I had hatched it for the air,
And rightly came from that brave mounting brood;
And when the plumes were summed with sweet desire,
To prove the pinions it ascends the skies;
Do what I could, it needsly would aspire
To my soul's sun, those two celestial eyes.
    Thus from my breast, where it was bred alone,
    It after thee is like an eaglet flown.

LVII

You best discerned of my mind's inward eyes,
And yet your graces outwardly divine,
Whose dear remembrance in my bosom lies,
Too rich a relic for so poor a shrine;
You, in whom nature chose herself to view,
When she her own perfection would admire;
Bestowing all her excellence on you,
At whose pure eyes Love lights his hallowed fire;
Even as a man that in some trance hath seen
More than his wond'ring utterance can unfold,
That rapt in spirit in better worlds hath been,
So must your praise distractedly be told;
    Most of all short when I would show you most,
    In your perfections so much am I lost.

LVIII

In former times, such as had store of coin,
In wars at home or when for conquests bound,
For fear that some their treasure should purloin,
Gave it to keep to spirits within the ground;
And to attend it them as strongly tied
Till they returned. Home when they never came,
Such as by art to get the same have tried,
From the strong spirit by no means force the same.
Nearer men come, that further flies away,
Striving to hold it strongly in the deep.
Ev'n as this spirit, so you alone do play
With those rich beauties Heav'n gives you to keep;
    Pity so left to th' coldness of your blood,
    Not to avail you nor do others good.

TO PROVERBS

LIX

As Love and I late harboured in one inn,
With Proverbs thus each other entertain.
'In love there is no lack,' thus I begin:
'Fair words make fools,' replieth he again.
'Who spares to speak, doth spare to speed,' quoth I.
'As well,' saith he, 'too forward as too slow.'
'Fortune assists the boldest,' I reply.
'A hasty man,' quoth he, 'ne'er wanted woe!'
'Labour is light, where love,' quoth I, 'doth pay.'
Saith he, 'Light burden's heavy, if far born.'
Quoth I, 'The main lost, cast the by away!'
'You have spun a fair thread,' he replies in scorn.
    And having thus awhile each other thwarted,
    Fools as we met, so fools again we parted.

LX

Define my weal, and tell the joys of heaven;
Express my woes and show the pains of hell;
Declare what fate unlucky stars have given,
And ask a world upon my life to dwell;
Make known the faith that fortune could no move,
Compare my worth with others' base desert,
Let virtue be the touchstone of my love,
So may the heavens read wonders in my heart;
Behold the clouds which have eclipsed my sun,
And view the crosses which my course do let;
Tell me, if ever since the world begun
So fair a rising had so foul a set?
    And see if time, if he would strive to prove,
    Can show a second to so pure a love.

LXI

Since there's no help, come let us kiss and part,
Nay I have done, you get no more of me;
And I am glad, yea glad with all my heart,
That thus so cleanly I myself can free;
Shakes hands for ever, cancel all our vows,
And when we meet at any time again,
Be it not seen in either of our brows
That we one jot of former love retain.
Now at the last gasp of Love's latest breath,
When his pulse failing, Passion speechless lies,
When Faith is kneeling by his bed of death,
And Innocence is closing up his eyes:
    Now if thou wouldst, when all have given him over,
    From death to life thou might'st him yet recover!

LXII

When first I ended, then I first began;
Then more I travelled further from my rest.
Where most I lost, there most of all I won;
Pinèd with hunger, rising from a feast.
Methinks I fly, yet want I legs to go,
Wise in conceit, in act a very sot,
Ravished with joy amidst a hell of woe,
What most I seem that surest am I not.
I build my hopes a world above the sky,
Yet with the mole I creep into the earth;
In plenty I am starved with penury,
And yet I surfeit in the greatest dearth.
    I have, I want, despair, and yet desire,
    Burned in a sea of ice, and drowned amidst a fire.

LXIII

Truce, gentle Love, a parley now I crave,
Methinks 'tis long since first these wars begun;
Nor thou, nor I, the better yet can have;
Bad is the match where neither party won.
I offer free conditions of fair peace,
My heart for hostage that it shall remain.
Discharge our forces, here let malice cease,
So for my pledge thou give me pledge again.
Or if no thing but death will serve thy turn,
Still thirsting for subversion of my state,
Do what thou canst, raze, massacre, and burn;
Let the world see the utmost of thy hate;
    I send defiance, since if overthrown,
    Thou vanquishing, the conquest is mine own.

Amoretti

EDMUND SPENSER

(*c.* 1552-1599)

I

Happy, ye leaves! when as those lilly hands
Which hold my life in their dead-doing might
Shall handle you, and hold in loves soft bands,
Lyke captives trembling at the victors sight.
And happy lines! on which, with starry light.
Those lamping eyes will deigne sometimes to look,
And reade the sorrowes of my dying spright,
And happy rymes! bath'd in the sacred brooke
Of Helicon, whence she derived is.
When ye behold that Angels blessed looke,
My soules long-lacked food, my heavens blis,
    Leaves, lines, and rymes, seeke her to please alone,
    Whom if ye please, I care for other none!

II

Unquiet thought! whom at the first I bred
Of th'inward bale of my love-pined hart,
And sithens have with sighes and sorrowes fed,
Till greater then my wombe thou woxen art,
Breake forth at length out of the inner part,
In which thou lurkest lyke to vipers brood,
And seeke some succour both to ease my smart,
And also to sustayne thy selfe with food.
But if in presence of that fayrest Proud
Thou chance to come, fall lowly at her feet;
And with meek humblesse and afflicted mood
Pardon for thee, and grace for me, intreat:
   Which if she graunt, then live, and my love cherish:
   If not, die soone, and I with thee will perish.

III

The soverayne beauty which I do admyre,
Witnesse the world how worthy to be prayzed!
The light wherof hath kindled heavenly fyre
In my fraile spirit, by her from basenesse raysed;
That being now with her huge brightnesse dazed,
Base thing I can no more endure to view:
But, looking still on her, I stand amazed
At wondrous sight of so celestiall hew.
So when my toung would speak her praises dew,
It stopped is with thoughts astonishment;
And when my pen would write her titles true,
It ravisht is with fancies wonderment:
   Yet in my hart I then both speak and write
   The wonder that my wit cannot endite.

IV

New yeare, forth looking out of Ianus gate,
Doth seeme to promise hope of new delight,
And, bidding th'old adieu, his passed date
Bids all old thoughts to die in dumpish spright;
And calling forth out of sad Winters night
Fresh Love, that long hath slept in cheerlesse bower,
Wils him awake, and soone about him dight
His wanton wings and darts of deadly power.
For lusty Spring now in his timely howre
Is ready to come forth, him to receive;
And warns the Earth with divers colord flowre
To decke hir selfe, and her faire mantle weave.
    Then you, faire flowre! in whom fresh youth doth
                                        raine,
    Prepare your selfe new love to entertaine.

V

Rudely thou wrongest my deare harts desire,
In finding fault with her too portly pride:
The thing which I doo most in her admire,
Is of the world unworthy most envide.
For in those lofty lookes is close implide
Scorn of base things, and sdeigne of foul dishonor;
Thretning rash eyes which gaze on her so wide,
That loosely they ne dare to looke upon her.
Such pride is praise, such portlinesse is honor,
That boldned innocence beares in hir eyes,
And her faire countenaunce, like a goodly banner,
Spreds in defiaunce of all enemies.
  Was never in this world ought worthy tride,
  Without some spark of such self-pleasing pride.

VI

Be nought dismayd that her unmoved mind
Doth still persist in her rebellious pride:
Such love, not lyke to lusts of baser kynd,
The harder wonne, the firmer will abide.
The durefull oake whose sap is not yet dride
Is long ere it conceive the kindling fyre;
But when it once doth burne, it doth divide
Great heat, and makes his flames to heaven aspire.
So hard it is to kindle new desire
In gentle brest, that shall endure for ever:
Deepe is the wound that dints the parts entire
With chaste affects, that naught but death can sever.
  Then thinke not long in taking litle paine
  To knit the knot that ever shall remaine.

VII

Fayre eyes! the myrrour of my mazed hart,
What wondrous vertue is contayn'd in you,
The which both lyfe and death forth from you dart
Into the obiect of your mighty view?
For when ye mildly looke with lovely hew,
Then is my soule with life and love inspired:
But when ye lowre, or looke on me askew,
Then do I die, as one with lightning fyred.
But since that lyfe is more then death desyred,
Looke ever lovely, as becomes you best;
That your bright beams, of my weak eyes admyred,
May kindle living fire within my brest.
    Such life should be the honor of your light,
    Such death the sad ensample of your might.

VIII

More then most faire, full of the living fire
Kindled above unto the Maker nere,
No eyes, but joyes, in which al powers conspire,
That to the world naught else be counted deare!
Thrugh your bright beames doth not the blinded guest
Shoot out his darts to base affections wound;
But angels come, to lead fraile mindes to rest
In chast desires, on heavenly beauty bound.
You frame my thoughts, and fashion me within;
You stop my toung, and teach my hart to speake;
You calme the storme that passion did begin,
Strong thrugh your cause, but by your vertue weak.
  Dark is the world where your light shined never;
  Well is he borne that may behold you ever.

IX

Long-while I sought to what I might compare
Those powrefull eyes which lighten my dark spright;
Yet find I nought on earth, to which I dare
Resemble th'ymage of their goodly light.
Not to the sun, for they doo shine by night;
Nor to the moone, for they are changed never;
Nor to the starres, for they have purer sight;
Nor to the fire, for they consume not ever;
Nor to the lightning, for they still persever;
Nor to the diamond, for they are more tender;
Nor unto cristall, for nought may them sever;
Nor unto glasse, such basenesse mought offend her.
   Then to the Maker selfe they likest be,
    Whose light doth lighten all that here we see.

X

Unrighteous Lord of love, what law is this,
That me thou makest thus tormented be,
The whiles she lordeth in licentious blisse
Of her freewill, scorning both thee and me?
See! how the Tyrannesse doth joy to see
The hugh massacres which her eyes do make,
And humbled harts brings captive unto thee,
That thou of them mayst mightie vengeance take.
But her proud hart doe thou a little shake,
And that high look, with which she doth comptroll
All this worlds pride, bow to a baser make,
And al her faults in thy black booke enroll:
   That I may laugh at her in equall sort
    As she doth laugh at me, and makes my pain her
                  sport.

XI

Dayly when I do seeke and sew for peace,
And hostages doe offer for ray truth,
She, cruell warriour, doth her selfe addresse
To battell, and the weary war renew'th;
Ne wilbe moov'd, with reason or with rewth,
To graunt small respit to my restlesse toile;
But greedily her fell intent poursewth,
Of my poore life to make unpittied spoile.
Yet my poore life, all sorrowes to assoyle,
I would her yield, her wrath to pacify;
But then she seeks, with torment and turmoyle,
To force me live, and will not let me dy.
   All paine hath end, and every war hafh peace;
   But mine, no price nor prayer may surcease.

XII

One day I sought with her hart-thrilling eyes
To make a truce, and termes to entertaine;
All fearlesse then of so false enimies,
Which sought me to entrap in treasons traine.
So, as I then disarmed did remaine,
A wicked ambush, which lay hidden long
In the close covert of her guilful eyen,
Thence breaking forth, did thick about me throng.
Too feeble I t'dabide the brunt so strong,
Was forst to yield my selfe into their hands;
Who, me captiving streight with rigorous wrong,
Have ever since kept me in cruell bands.
  So, Ladie, now to you I doo complaine
  Against your eyes, that iustice I may gaine.

XIII

In that proud port which her so goodly graceth,
Whiles her faire face she reares up to the skie,
And to the ground her eie-lids low embaseth,
Most goodly temperature ye may descry;
Myld humblesse mixt with awful! maiestie.
For, looking on the earth whence she was borne,
Her minde remembreth her mortalitie,
Whatso is fayrest shall to earth returne.
But that same lofty countenance seemes to scorne
Base thing, and thinke how she to heaven may clime;
Treading downe earth as lothsome and forlorne,
That hinders heavenly thoughts with drossy slime.
    Yet lowly still vouchsafe to looke on me;
    Such lowlinesse shall make you lofty be.

XIV

Retourne agayne, my forces late dismayd,
Unto the siege by you abandon'd quite.
Great shame it is to leave, like one afrayd,
So fayre a peece for one repulse so light.
'dGaynst such strong castles needeth greater might
Then those small forts which ye were wont belay:
Such haughty mynds, enur'd to hardy fight,
Disdayne to yield unto the first assay.
Bring therefore all the forces that ye may,
And lay incessant battery to her heart;
Playnts, prayers, vowes, ruth, sorrow, and dismay;
Those engins can the proudest love convert:
  And, if those fayle, fall down and dy before her;
  So dying live, and living do adore her.

XV

Ye tradefull Merchants, that, with weary toyle,
Do seeke most pretious things to make your gain,
And both the Indias of their treasure spoile,
What needeth you to seeke so farre in vaine?
For loe, my Love doth in her selfe containe
All this worlds riches that may farre be found:
If saphyres, loe, her eyes be saphyres plaine;
If rubies, loe, hir lips be rubies sound;
If pearles, hir teeth be pearles, both pure and round;
If yvorie, her forhead yvory weene;
If gold, her locks are finest gold on ground;
If silver, her faire hands are silver sheene:
   But that which fairest is but few behold:-
   Her mind adornd with vertues manifold.

XVI

One day as I unwarily did gaze
On those fayre eyes, my loves immortall light,
The whiles my stonisht hart stood in amaze,
Through sweet illusion of her lookes delight,
I mote perceive how, in her glauncing sight,
Legions of Loves with little wings did fly,
Darting their deadly arrows, fyry bright,
At every rash beholder passing by.
One of those archers closely I did spy,
Ayming his arrow at my very hart:
When suddenly, with twincle of her eye,
The damzell broke his misintended dart.
   Had she not so doon, sure I had bene slayne;
   Yet as it was, I hardly scap'dt with paine.

XVII

The glorious pourtraict of that angels face,
Made to amaze weake mens confused skil,
And this worlds worthlesse glory to embase,
What pen, what pencil!, can expresse her fill?
For though he colours could devize at will,
And eke his learned hand at pleasure guide,
Least, trembling, it his workmanship should spill,
Yet many wondrous things there are beside:
The sweet eye-glaunces, that like arrowes glide,
The charming smiles, that rob sence from the hart,
The lovely pleasance, and the lofty pride,
Cannot expressed be by any art.
　　A greater craftesmans hand thereto doth neede,
　　That can expresse the life of things indeed.

XVIII

The rolling wheele that runneth often round,
The hardest steele, in tract of time doth teare:
And drizling drops, that often doe redound,
The firmest flint doth in continuance weare:
Yet cannot I, with many a drooping teare
And long intreaty, soften her hard hart,
That she will once vouchsafe my plaint to heare,
Or looke with pitty on my payneful smart.
But when I pleade, she bids me play my part;
And when I weep, she sayes, teares are but water;
And when I sigh, she sayes, I know the art;
And when I waile, she turnes hir selfe to laughter.
  So do I weepe, and wayle, and pleade in vaine,
  Whiles she as steele and flint doth still remayne.

XIX

The merry cuckow, messenger of Spring,
His trompet shrill hath thrise already sounded.
That warnes al lovers wayte upon their king,
Who now is coming forth with girland crouned.
With noyse whereof the quyre of byrds resounded
Their anthemes sweet, devized of loves prayse,
That all the woods theyr ecchoes back rebounded,
As if they knew the meaning of their layes.
But mongst them all which did Loves honor rayse,
No word was heard of her that most it ought;
But she his precept proudly disobayes,
And doth his ydle message set at nought.
   Therefore, O Love, unlesse she turne to thee
   Ere cuckow end, let her a rebell be!

XX

In vaine I seeke and sew to her for grace,
And doe myne humbled hart before her poure,
The whiles her foot she in my necke doth place,
And tread my life downe in the lowly floure.
And yet the lyon, that is lord of power,
And reigneth over every beast in field,
In his most pride disdeigneth to devoure
The silly lambe that to his might doth yield.
But she, more cruell and more salvage wylde
Than either lyon or the lyonesse,
Shames not to be with guiltlesse bloud defylde,
But taketh glory in her cruelnesse.
  Fayrer then fayrest! let none ever say
  That ye were blooded in a yeelded pray.

XXI

Was it the worke of Nature or of Art,
Which tempred so the feature of her face,
That pride and meeknesse, mist by equall part,
Doe both appeare t'dadorne her beauties grace?
For with mild pleasance, which doth pride displace,
She to her love doth lookers eyes allure;
And with stern countenance back again doth chace
Their looser lookes that stir up lustes impure.
With such strange termes her eyes she doth inure,
That with one looke she doth my life dismay,
And with another doth it streight recure:
Her smile me drawes; her frowne me drives away.
  Thus doth she traine and teach me with her lookes;
  Such art of eyes I never read in bookes!

XXII

This holy season, fit to fast and pray,
Men to devotion ought to be inclynd:
Therefore, I lykewise, on so holy day,
For my sweet saynt some service fit will find.
Her temple fayre is built within my mind,
In which her glorious ymage placed is;
On which my thoughts doo day and night attend,
Lyke sacred priests that never thinke amisse.
There I to her, as th'dauthor of my blisse,
Will builde an altar to appease her yre;
And on the same my hart will sacrifise,
Burning in flames of pure and chaste desyre:
  The which vouchsafe, O Goddesse, to accept,
  Amongst thy deerest relicks to be kept.

XXIII

Penelope, for her Ulisses sake,
Deviz'd a web her wooers to deceave;
In which the worke that she all day did make,
The same at night she did againe unreave.
Such subtile craft my damzell doth conceave,
Th'dimportune suit of my desire to shonne:
For all that I in many dayes do weave,
In one short houre I find by her undonne.
So when I thinke to end that I begonne,
I must begin and never bring to end:
For with one looke she spils that long I sponne,
And with one word my whole years work doth rend.
   Such labour like the spyders web I fynd,
   Whose fruitlesse worke is broken with least wynd.

XXIV

When I behold that beauties wonderment,
And rare perfection of each goodly part,
Of Natures skill the onely complement,
I honor and admire the Makers art.
But when I feele the bitter balefull smart
Which her fayre eyes unwares doe worke in mee,
That death out of theyr shiny beames doe dart,
I thinke that I a new Pandora see,
Whom all the gods in councell did agree
Into this sinfull world from heaven to send,
That she to wicked men a scourge should bee,
For all their faults with which they did offend.
  But since ye are my scourge, I will intreat
  That for my faults ye will me gently beat.

XXV

How long shall this lyke-dying lyfe endure,
And know no end of her owne mysery,
But wast and weare away in termes unsure,
'dTwixt feare and hope depending doubtfully!
Yet better were attonce to let me die,
And shew the last ensample of your pride,
Then to torment me thus with cruelty,
To prove your powre, which I too wel have tride.
But yet if in your hardned brest ye bide
A close intent at last to shew me grace,
Then all the woes and wrecks which I abide,
As meanes of blisse I gladly wil embrace;
    And wish that more and greater they might be,
    That greater meede at last may turne to mee.

XXVI

Sweet is the rose, but growes upon a brere;
Sweet is the junipeer; but sharpe his bough;
Sweet is the eglantine, but pricketh nere;
Sweet is the firbloome, but his braunches rough;
Sweet is the cypresse, but his rynd is rough;
Sweet is the nut, but bitter is his pill;
Sweet is the broome-flowre, but yet sowre enough;
And sweet is moly, but his root is ill.
So every sweet with soure is tempred still,
That maketh it be coveted the more:
For easie things, that may be got at will,
Most sorts of men doe set but little store.
  Why then should I accompt of little paine,
  That endlesse pleasure shall unto me gaine!

XXVII

Faire Proud! now tell me, why should faire be proud,
Sith all worlds glorie is but drosse uncleane,
And in the shade of death it selfe shall shroud,
However now thereof ye little weene!
That goodly idoll, now so gay beseene,
Shall doffe her fleshes borrowd fayre attyre,
And be forgot as it had never beene,
That many now much worship and admire!
Ne any then shall after it inquire,
Ne any mention shall thereof remaine,
But what this verse, that never shall expyre,
Shall to you purchas with her thankles pain!
  Faire! be no lenger proud of that shall perish,
  But that which shall you make immortall cherish.

XVIII

The laurel-leafe which you this day doe weare
Gives me great hope of your relenting mynd:
For since it is the badge which I doe beare,
Ye, bearing it, doe seeme to me inclind.
The powre thereof, which ofte in me I find,
Let it likewise your gentle brest inspire
With sweet infusion, and put you in mind
Of that proud mayd whom now those leaves attyre:
Proud Daphne, scorning Phrebus lovely fyre,
On the Thessalian shore from him did flie;
For which the gods, in theyr revengefull yre,
Did her transforme into a laurell-tree.
    Then fly no more, fayre Love, from Phebus chace,
    But in your brest his leafe and love embrace.

XXIX

See! how the stubborne damzell doth deprave
My simple meaning with disdaynfull scorne,
And by the bay which I unto her gave
Accoumpts my self her captive quite forlorne.
The bay, quoth she, is of the victours born,
Yielded them by the vanquisht as theyr meeds,
And they therewith doe poetes heads adorne,
To sing the glory of their famous deeds.
But sith she will the conquest challeng needs,
Let her accept me as her faithfull thrall;
That her great triumph, which my skill exceeds,
I may in trump of fame blaze over all.
   Then would I decke her head with glorious bayes,
   And fill the world with her victorious prayse.

XXX

My Love is lyke to yse, and I to fyre:
How comes it then that this her cold so great
Is not dissolv'd through my so hot desyre,
But harder growes the more I her intreat?
Or how comes it that my exceeding heat
Is not delayd by her hart-frosen cold,
But that I burne much more in boyling sweat,
And feele my flames augmented manifold?
What more miraculous thing may be told,
That fire, which all things melts, should harden yse,
And yse, which is congeald with sencelesse cold,
Should kindle fyre by wonderful devyse?
   Such is the powre of love in gentle mind,
   That it can alter all the course of kynd.

XXXI

Ah! why hath Nature to so hard a hart
Given so goodly giftes of beauties grace,
Whose pryde depraves each other better part,
And all those pretious ornaments deface?
Sith to all other beastes of bloody race
A dreadfull countenance she given hath,
That with theyr terrour all the rest may chace,
And warne to shun the daunger of theyr wrath.
But my proud one doth worke the greater scath,
Through sweet allurement of her lovely hew,
That she the better may in bloody bath
Of such poore thralls her cruell hands embrew.
  But did she know how ill these two accord,
  Such cruelty she would have soone abhord.

XXXII

The paynefull smith with force of fervent heat
The hardest yron soone doth mollify,
That with his heavy sledge he can it beat,
And fashion to what he it list apply.
Yet cannot all these flames in which I fry
Her hart, more hard then yron, soft a whit,
Ne all the playnts and prayers with which I
Doe beat on th'dandvile of her stubberne wit:
But still, the more she fervent sees my fit,
The more she frieseth in her wilfull pryde,
And harder growes, the harder she is smit
With all the playnts which to her be applyde.
　　What then remaines but I to ashes burne,
　　And she to stones at length all frosen turne!

XXXIII

Great wrong I doe, I can it not deny,
To that most sacred empresse, my dear dred,
Not finishing her Queene of Faery,
That mote enlarge her living prayses, dead.
But Lodwick, this of grace to me aread:
Do ye not thinck th'daccomplishment of it
Sufficient worke for one mans simple head,
All were it, as the rest, but rudely writ?
How then should I, without another wit,
Thinck ever to endure so tedious toyle,
Sith that this one is tost with troublous fit
Of a proud Love, that doth my spirite spoyle?
  Cease, then, till she vouchsafe to grawnt me rest,
  Or lend you me another living brest.

XXXIV

Lyke as a ship, that through the ocean wyde
By conduct of some star doth make her way,
Whenas a storm hath dimd her trusty guyde,
Out of her course doth wander far astray,
So I, whose star, that wont with her bright ray
Me to direct, with cloudes is over-cast,
Doe wander now in darknesse and dismay,
Through hidden perils round about me plast.
Yet hope I well that, when this storme is past,
My Helice, the lodestar of ray lyfe,
Will shine again, and looke on me at last,
With lovely light to cleare my cloudy grief.
  Till then I wander carefull, comfortlesse,
  In secret sorrow and sad pensivenesse.

XXXV

My hungry eyes, through greedy covetize
Still to behold the obiect of their paine,
With no contentment can themselves suffize;
But having, pine, and having not, complaine.
For lacking it, they cannot lyfe sustayne;
And having it, they gaze on it the more,
In their amazement lyke Narcissus vaine,
Whose eyes him starv'd: so plenty makes me poore.
Yet are mine eyes so filled with the store
Of that faire sight, that nothing else they brooke,
But lothe the things which they did like before,
And can no more endure on them to looke.
   All this worlds glory seemeth vayne to me,
    And all their showes but shadowes, saving she.

XXXVI

Tell me, when shall these wearie woes have end;
Or shall their ruthlesse torment never cease,
But al my days in pining languor spend,
Without hope of asswagement or release?
Is there no meanes for me to purchace peace,
Or make agreement with her thrilling eyes;
But that their cruelty doth still increace,
And dayly more augment my miseryes?
But when ye have shew'd all extremityes,
Then think how little glory ye have gayned
By slaying him, whose lyfe, though ye despyse,
Mote have your life in honor long maintayned.
  But by his death, which some perhaps will mone,
  Ye shall condemned be of many a one.

XXXVII

What guyle is this, that those her golden tresses
She doth attyre under a net of gold,
And with sly skill so cunningly them dresses,
That which is gold or haire may scarse be told?
Is it that mens frayle eyes, which gaze too bold,
She may entangle in that golden snare;
And, being caught, may craftily enfold
Their weaker harts, which are not wel aware?
Take heed therefore, myne eyes, how ye doe stare
Henceforth too rashly on that guilefull net,
In which if ever ye entrapped are,
Out of her bands ye by no meanes shall get.
    Fondnesse it were for any, being free,
    To covet fetters, though they golden bee!

XXXVIII

Arion, when, through tempests cruel wracke,
He forth was thrown into the greedy seas,
Through the sweet musick which his harp did make
Allur'd a dolphin him from death to ease.
But my rude musick, which was wont to please
Some dainty eares, cannot, with any skill,
The dreadfull tempest of her wrath appease,
Nor move the dolphin from her stubborn will.
But in her pride she dooth persever still,
All carelesse how my life for her decayes:
Yet with one word she can it save or spill.
To spill were pitty, but to save were prayse!
  Chuse rather to be praysd for doing good,
   Then to be blam'd for spilling guiltlesse blood.

XXXIX

Sweet smile! the daughter of the Queene of Love,
Expressing all thy mothers powrefull art,
With which she wonts to temper angry Iove,
When all the gods he threats with thundring dart,
Sweet is thy vertue, as thy selfe sweet art.
For when on me thou shinedst late in sadnesse,
A melting pleasance ran through every part,
And me revived with hart-robbing gladnesse;
Whylest rapt with joy resembling heavenly madness,
My soule was ravisht quite as in a traunce,
And, feeling thence no more her sorrowes sadnesse,
Fed on the fulnesse of that chearfull glaunce.
  More sweet than nectar, or ambrosiall meat,
  Seem'd every bit which thenceforth I did eat.

XL

Mark when she smiles with amiable cheare,
And tell me whereto can ye lyken it;
When on each eyelid sweetly doe appeare
An hundred Graces as in shade to sit.
Lykest it seemeth, in my simple wit,
Unto the fayre sunshine in somers day,
That, when a dreadfull storme away is flit,
Thrugh the broad world doth spred his goodly ray
At sight whereof, each bird that sits on spray.
And every beast that to his den was fled,
Comes forth afresh out of their late dismay,
And to the light lift up their drouping hed.
   So my storme-beaten hart likewise is cheared
   With that sunshine, when cloudy looks are cleared.

XLI

Is it her nature, or is it her will,
To be so cruell to an humbled foe?
If nature, then she may it mend with skill;
If will, then she at will may will forgoe.
But if her nature and her will be so,
That she will plague the man that loves her most,
And take delight t'encrease a wretches woe,
Then all her natures goodly guifts are lost;
And that same glorious beauties ydle boast
Is but a bayt such wretches to beguile,
As, being long in her loves tempest tost,
She meanes at last to make her pitious spoyle.
  O fayrest fayre! let never it be named,
  That so fayre beauty was so fowly shamed.

XLII

The love which me so cruelly tormenteth
So pleasing is in my extreamest paine,
That, all the more my sorrow it augmenteth,
The more I love and doe embrace my bane.
Ne do I wish (for wishing were but vaine)
To be acquit fro my continual smart,
But joy her thrall for ever to remayne,
And yield for pledge my poor and captyved hart,
The which, that it from her may never start,
Let her, yf please her, bynd with adamant chayne,
And from all wandring loves, which mote pervart
His safe assurance, strongly it restrayne.
  Onely let her abstaine from cruelty,
  And doe me not before my time to dy.

XLIII

Shall I then silent be, or shall I speake?
And if I speake, her wrath renew I shall;
And if I silent be, my hart will breake,
Or choked be with overflowing gall.
What tyranny is this, both my hart to thrall,
And eke my toung with proud restraint to tie,
That neither I may speake nor thinke at all,
But like a stupid stock in silence die!
Yet I my hart with silence secretly
Will teach to speak and my just cause to plead,
And eke mine eyes, with meek humility,
Love-learned letters to her eyes to read;
   Which her deep wit, that true harts thought can
                         spel,
   Wil soon conceive, and learne to construe well.

XLIV

When those renoumed noble peres of Greece
Through stubborn pride among themselves did iar,
Forgetfull of the famous golden fleece,
Then Orpheus with his harp theyr strife did bar.
But this continuall, cruell, civill warre
The which my selfe against my selfe doe make,
Whilest my weak powres of passions warreid arre,
No skill can stint, nor reason can aslake.
But when in hand my tunelesse harp I take,
Then doe I more augment my foes despight,
And griefe renew, and passions doe awake
To battaile, fresh against my selfe to fight.
  Mongst whome the more I seeke to settle peace,
  The more I fynd their malice to increace.

XLV

Leave, Lady! in your glasse of cristall clene
Your goodly selfe for evermore to vew,
And in my selfe, (my inward selfe I meane,)
Most lively lyke behold your semblant trew.
Within my hart, though hardly it can shew
Thing so divine to vew of earthly eye,
The fayre idea of your celestiall hew
And every part remaines immortally:
And were it not that through your cruelty
With sorrow dimmed and deform'd it were,
The goodly ymage of your visnomy,
Clearer than cristall, would therein appere.
  But if your selfe in me ye playne will see,
  Remove the cause by which your fayre beames
                          darkned be.

XLVI

When my abodes prefixed time is spent,
My cruell fayre streight bids me wend my way:
But then from heaven most hideous stormes are sent,
As willing me against her will to stay.
Whom then shall I-or heaven, or her-obay?
The heavens know best what is the best for me:
But as she will, whose will my life doth sway,
My lower heaven, so it perforce must be.
But ye high hevens, that all this sorowe see,
Sith all your tempests cannot hold me backe,
Aswage your storms, or else both you and she
Will both together me too sorely wrack.
  Enough it is for one man to sustaine
  The stormes which she alone on me doth raine.

XLVII

Trust not the treason of those smyling lookes,
Untill ye have their guylefull traynes well tryde;
For they are lyke but unto golden hookes,
That from the foolish fish theyr bayts do hyde:
So she with flattring smyles weake harts doth guyde
Unto her love, and tempte to theyr decay;
Whome, being caught, she kills with cruell pryde,
And feeds at pleasure on the wretched pray.
Yet even whylst her bloody hands them slay,
Her eyes looke lovely, and upon them smyle,
That they take pleasure in their cruell play,
And, dying, doe themselves of payne beguyle.
   O mighty charm! which makes men love theyr bane,
   And thinck they dy with pleasure, live with payne.

XLVIII

Innocent paper! whom too cruell hand
Did make the matter to avenge her yre,
And ere she could thy cause well understand,
Did sacrifize unto the greedy fyre,
Well worthy thou to have found better hyre
Then so bad end, for hereticks ordayned;
Yet heresy nor treason didst conspire,
But plead thy maisters cause, unjustly payned:
Whom she, all carelesse of his grief, constrayned
To utter forth the anguish of his hart,
And would not heare, when he to her complayned
The piteous passion of his dying smart.
  Yet live for ever, though against her will,
  And speake her good, though she requite it ill.

XLIX

Fayre Cruell! why are ye so fierce and cruell?
Is it because your eyes have powre to kill?
Then know that mercy is the Mighties iewell,
And greater glory think to save then spill.
But if it be your pleasure and proud will
To shew the powre of your imperious eyes,
Then not on him that never thought you ill,
But bend your force against your enemyes.
Let them feel the utmost of your crueltyes,
And kill with looks, as cockatrices do:
But him that at your footstoole humbled lies,
With mercifull regard give mercy to.
  Such mercy shall you make admyr'd to be;
  So shall you live, by giving life to me.

L

Long languishing in double malady
Of my harts wound and of my bodies griefe,
There came to me a leach, that would apply
Fit medcines for my bodies best reliefe.
Vayne man, quoth I, that hast but little priefe
In deep discovery of the mynds disease;
Is not the hart of all the body chiefe,
And rules the members as it selfe doth please?
Then with some cordialls seeke for to appease
The inward languor of my wounded hart,
And then my body shall have shortly ease.
But such sweet cordialls passe physicians art:
  Then, my lyfes leach! doe you your skill reveale,
  And with one salve both hart and body heale.

LI

Doe I not see that fayrest ymages
Of hardest marble are of purpose made,
For that they should endure through many ages,
Ne let theyr famous moniments to fade?
Why then doe I, untrainde in lovers trade,
Her hardnes blame, which I should more commend?
Sith never ought was excellent assayde
Which was not hard t'datchive and bring to end;
Ne ought so hard, but he that would attend
Mote soften it and to his will allure.
So do I hope her stubborne hart to bend,
And that it then more stedfast will endure:
    Only my paines wil be the more to get her;
    But, having her, my joy wil be the greater.

LII

So oft as homeward I from her depart,
I go lyke one that, having lost the field,
Is prisoner led away with heavy hart,
Despoyld of warlike armes and knowen shield.
So doe I now my self a prisoner yield
To sorrow and to solitary paine,
From presence of my dearest deare exylde,
Long-while alone in languor to remaine.
There let no thought of joy, or pleasure vaine,
Dare to approch, that may my solace breed;
Bet sudden dumps, and drery sad disdayne
Of all worlds gladnesse, more my torment feed.
  So I her absens will my penaunce make,
  That of her presens I my meed may take.

LIII

The panther, knowing that his spotted hyde
Doth please all beasts, but that his looks them fray,
Within a bush his dreadful head doth hide,
To let them gaze, whylst he on them may pray.
Right so my cruell fayre with me doth play;
For with the goodly semblance of her hew
She doth allure me to mine owne decay,
And then no mercy will unto me shew.
Great shame it is, thing so divine in view,
Made for to be the worlds most ornament,
To make the bayte her gazers to embrew:
Good shames to be to ill an instrument!
   But mercy doth with beautie best agree,
   As in theyr Maker ye them best may see.

LIV

Of this worlds theatre in which we stay,
My Love, like the spectator, ydly sits,
Beholding me, that all the pageants play,
Disguysing diversly my troubled wits.
Sometimes I joy when glad occasion fits,
And mask in myrth lyke to a comedy:
Soone after, when my joy to sorrow flits,
I waile, and make my woes a tragedy.
Yet she, beholding me with constant eye,
Delights not in my merth, nor rues my smart:
But when I laugh, she mocks; and when I cry,
She laughs, and hardens evermore her hart.
   What then can move her? If nor merth, nor mone,
   She is no woman, but a sencelesse stone.

LV

So oft as I her beauty doe behold,
And therewith doe her cruelty compare,
I marvaile of what substance was the mould
The which her made attonce so cruell faire.
Not earth; for her high thoughts more heavenly are:
Not water; for her love doth burne like fyre:
Not ayre; for she is not so light or rare;
Not fyre; for she doth friese with faint desire.
Then needs another element inquire,
Whereof she mote be made; that is, the skye.
For to the heaven her haughty looks aspire,
And eke her love is pure immortall hye.
   Then sith to heaven ye lykened are the best,
   Be lyke in mercy as in all the rest.

LVI

Fayre ye be sure, but cruell and unkind,
As is a tygre, that with greedinesse
Hunts after bloud; when he by chance doth find
A feeble beast, doth felly him oppresse.
Fayre be ye sure, but proud and pitilesse,
As is a storme, that all things doth prostrate;
Finding a tree alone all comfortlesse,
Beats on it strongly, it to ruinate.
Fayre be ye sure, but hard and obstinate,
As is a rocke amidst the raging floods;
Gaynst which a ship, of succour desolate,
Doth suffer wreck both of her selfe and goods.
  That ship, that tree, and that same beast, am I,
  Whom ye doe wreck, doe ruine, and destroy.

LVII

Sweet warriour! when shall I have peace with you?
High time it is this warre now ended were,
Which I no lenger can endure to sue,
Ne your incessant battry more to beare.
So weake my powres, so sore my wounds, appear,
That wonder is how I should live a iot,
Seeing my hart through-launced every where
With thousand arrowes which your eyes have shot.
Yet shoot ye sharpely still, and spare me not,
But glory thinke to make these cruel stoures.
Ye cruell one! what glory can be got,
In slaying him that would live gladly yours?
   Make peace therefore, and graunt me timely grace,
   That al my wounds will heale in little space.

LVIII

By her that is most assured to her selfe.
Weake is th'dassurance that weake flesh reposeth
In her own powre, and scorneth others ayde;
That soonest fals, when as she most supposeth
Her selfe assur'd, and is of nought affrayd,
All flesh is frayle, and all her strength unstayd,
Like a vaine bubble blowen up with ayre:
Devouring tyme and changeful chance have prayd
Her glorious pride, that none may it repayre.
Ne none so rich or wise, so strong or fayre,
But fayletb, trusting on his owne assurance:
And he that standeth on the hyghest stayre
Fals lowest; for on earth nought hath endurance.
  Why then doe ye, proud fayre, misdeeme so farre,
  That to your selfe ye most assured arre!

LIX

Thrise happie she that is so well assured
Unto her selfe, and setled so in hart,
That neither will for better be allured,
Ne feard with worse to any chaunce to start:
But, like a steddy ship, doth strongly part
The raging waves, and kcepes her course aright,
Ne ought for tempest doth from it depart,
Ne ought for fayrer weathers false delight.
Such selfe-assurance need not feare the spight
Of grudging foes, ne favour seek of friends:
But in the stay of her owne stedfast might,
Neither to one her selfe nor other bends.
    Most happy she that most assur'd doth rest;
    But he most happy who such one loves best.

LX

They that in course of heavenly spheares are skild
To every planet point his sundry yeare,
In which her circles voyage is fulfild:
As Mars in threescore yeares doth run his spheare.
So, since the winged god his planet cleare
Began in me to move, one yeare is spent;
The which doth longer unto me appeare,
Then al those fourty which my life out-went.
Then, by that count which lovers books invent,
The spheare of Cupid fourty yeares containes,
Which I have wasted in long languishment,
That seem'd the longer for my greater paines.
  But let my Loves fayre planet short her wayes
  This yeare ensuing, or else short my dayes.

LXI

The glorious image of the Makers beautie,
My soverayne saynt, the idoll of my thought,
Dare not henceforth, above the bounds of dewtie,
T'daccuse of pride, or rashly blame for ought.
For being, as she is, divinely wrought,
And of the brood of angels heavenly born,
And with the crew of blessed saynts upbrought,
Each of which did her with theyr guifts adorne,
The bud of joy, the blossome of the morne,
The beame of light, whom mortal eyes admyre,
What reason is it then but she should scorne
Base things, that to her love too bold aspire!
  Such heavenly formes ought rather worshipt be,
  Then dare be lov'd by men of meane degree.

LXII

The weary yeare his race now having run,
The new begins his compast course anew:
With shew of morning mylde he bath begun,
Betokening peace and plenty to ensew.
So let us, which this chaunge of weather vew,
Chaunge eke our mynds, and former lives amend;
The old yeares sinnes forepast let us eschew,
And fly the faults with which we did offend.
Then shall the new yeares joy forth freshly send
Into the glooming world his gladsome ray,
And all these stormes, which now his beauty blend,
Shall turne to calmes, and tymely cleare away.
  So, likewise, Love! cheare you your heavy spright,
  And chaunge old yeares annoy to new delight.

LXIII

After long stormes and tempests sad assay,
Which hardly I endured heretofore,
In dread of death, and daungerous dismay,
With which my silly bark was tossed sore,
I doe at length descry the happy shore,
In which I hope ere long for to arryve:
Fayre soyle it seemes from far, and fraught with store
Of all that deare and daynty is alyve.
Most happy he that can at last atchyve
The joyous safety of so sweet a rest;
Whose least delight sufficeth to deprive
Remembrance of all paines which him opprest.
   All paines are nothing in respect of this;
   All sorrowes short that gaine eternall blisse.

LXIV

Comming to kisse her lyps, (such grace I found,)
Me seemd I smelt a gardin of sweet flowres,
That dainty odours from them threw around,
For damzels fit to decke their lovers bowres.
Her lips did smell lyke unto gillyflowers;
Her ruddy cheekes lyke unto roses red;
Her snowy browes lyke budded bellamoures;
Her lovely eyes lyke pincks but newly spred;
Her goodly bosome lyke a strawberry bed;
Her neck lyke to a bounch of cullambynes;
Her brest lyke lillyes, ere their leaves be shed;
Her nipples lyke young blossomd jessemynes.
  Such fragrant flowres doe give most odorous smell;
  But her sweet odour did them all excell.

LXV

The doubt which ye misdeeme, fayre Love, is vaine,
That fondly feare to lose your liberty,
When, losing one, two liberties ye gayne,
And make him bond that bondage earst did fly.
Sweet be the bands the which true love doth tye,
Without constraynt or dread of any ill:
The gentle birde feeles no captivity
Within her cage, but sings, and feeds her fill.
There pride dare not approch, nor discord spill
The league twixt them that loyal love hath bound,
But simple Truth and mutual Good-will
Seeks with sweet peace to salve each others wound:
   There Fayth doth fearless dwell in brasen towre,
   And spotlesse Pleasure builds her sacred bowre.

LXVI

To all those happy blessings which ye have
With plenteous hand by heaven upon you thrown,
This one disparagement they to you gave,
That ye your love lent to so meane a one.
Ye, whose high worths surpassing paragon
Could not on earth have found one fit for mate,
Ne but in heaven matchable to none,
Why did ye stoup unto so lowly state?
But ye thereby much greater glory gate,
Then had ye sorted with a princes pere:
For now your light doth more it selfe dilate,
And, in my darknesse, greater doth appeare.
   Yet, since your light hath once enlumind me,
   With my reflex yours shall encreased be.

LXVII

Lyke as a huntsman, after weary chace,
Seeing the game from him escapt away,
Sits downe to rest him in some shady place,
With panting hounds, beguiled of their pray,
So, after long pursuit and vaine assay,
When I all weary had the chace forsooke,
The gentle deer returnd the selfe-same way,
Thinking to quench her thirst at the next brooke.
There she, beholding me with mylder looke,
Sought not to fly, but fearlesse still did bide,
Till I in hand her yet halfe trembling tooke,
And with her own goodwill her fyrmely tyde.
   Strange thing, me seemd, to see a beast so wyld
   So goodly wonne, with her owne will beguyld.

LXVIII

Most glorious Lord of lyfe! that on this day
Didst make thy triumph over death and sin,
And, having harrowd hell, didst bring away
Captivity thence captive, us to win,
This joyous day, dear Lord, with joy begin;
And grant that we, for whom thou diddest dy,
Being with thy deare blood clene washt from sin,
May live for ever in felicity;
And that thy love we weighing worthily,
May likewise love thee for the same againe,
And for thy sake, that all lyke deare didst buy.
With love may one another entertayne!
  So let us love, deare Love, lyke as we ought:
  Love is the lesson which the Lord us taught.

LXIX

The famous warriors of the anticke world
Us'd trophees to erect in stately wize,
In which they would the records have enrold
Of theyr great deeds and valorous emprize.
What trophee then shall I most fit devize,
In which I may record the memory
Of my loves conquest, peerlesse beauties prise,
Adorn'd with honour, love, and chastity!
Even this verse, vowd to eternity,
Shall be thereof immortall moniment,
And tell her praise to all posterity,
That may admire such worlds rare wonderment;
   The happy purchase of my glorious spoile,
   Gotten at last with labour and long toyle.

LXX

Fresh Spring, the herald of loves mighty king,
In whose cote-armour richly are displayd
All sorts of flowres the which on earth do spring,
In goodly colours gloriously arrayd,
Goe to my Love, where she is carelesse layd,
Yet in her winters bowre not well awake:
Tell her the joyous time wil not be staid,
Unlesse she doe him by the forelock take;
Bid her therefore her selfe soone ready make,
To wayt on Love amongst his lovely crew,
Where every one that misseth then her make
Shall be by him amearst with penance dew.
   Make haste therefore, sweet Love, while it is prime;
   For none can call againe the passed time.

LXXI

I joy to see how, in your drawen work,
Your selfe unto the Bee ye doe compare,
And me unto the Spyder, that doth lurke
In close awayt, to catch her unaware.
Right so your selfe were caught in cunning snare
Of a deare foe, and thralled to his love;
In whose streight bands ye now captived are
So firmely, that ye never may remove.
But as your worke is woven all about
With woodbynd flowers and fragrant eglantine,
So sweet your prison you in time shall prove,
With many deare delights bedecked fyne:
   And all thensforth eternall peace shall see
   Betweene the Spyder and the gentle Bee.

LXXII

Oft when my spirit doth spred her bolder winges,
In mind to mount up to the purest sky,
It down is weighd with thought of earthly things,
And clogd with burden of mortality:
Where, when that soverayne beauty it doth spy,
Resembling heavens glory in her light,
Drawn with sweet pleasures bayt it back doth fly,
And unto heaven forgets her former flight.
There my fraile fancy, fed with full delight,
Doth bathe in blisse, and mantlcth most at ease;
Ne thinks of other heaven, but how it might
Her harts desire with most contentment please.
   Hart need not wish none other happinesse,
   But here on earth to have such hevens blisse.

LXXIII

Being my self captyved here in care,
My hart, (whom none with servile bands can tye,
But the fayre tresses of your golden hayre,)
Breaking his prison, forth to you doth fly.
Like as a byrd, that in ones hand doth spy
Desired food, to it doth make his flight,
Even so my hart, that wont on your fayre eye
To feed his fill, flyes backe unto your sight.
Doe you him take, and in your bosome bright
Gently encage, that he may be your thrall:
Perhaps he there may learne, with rare delight,
To sing your name and prayses over all:
   That it hereafter may you not repent,
   Him lodging in your bosome to have lent.

LXXIV

Most happy letters! fram'd by skilfull trade,
With which that happy name was first desynd
The which three times thrise happy hath me made,
With guifts of body, fortune, and of mind.
The first ray being to me gave by kind,
From mothers womb deriv'd by dew descent:
The second is my sovereigne Queene most kind,
That honour and large richesse to me lent:
The third my Love, my lives last ornament,
By whom my spirit out of dust was raysed,
To speake her prayse and glory excellent,
Of all alive most worthy to be praysed.
   Ye three Elizabeths! for ever live,
   That three such graces did unto me give.

LXXV

One day I wrote her name upon the strand,
But came the waves and washed it away:
Agayne I wrote it with a second hand;
But came the tyde, and made my paynes his pray.
'Vayne man,' sayd she, 'that doest in vaine assay
A mortall thing so to immortalize;
For I my selve shall lyke to this decay,
And eke my name bee wyped out lykewize.'
'Not so,' quod I; 'let baser things devize
To dy in dust, but you shall live by fame:
My verse your vertues rare shall eternize,
And in the hevens wryte your glorious name.
   Where, when as death shall all the world subdew,
   Our love shall live, and later life renew.'

LXXVI

Fayre bosome! fraught with vertues richest tresure,
The neast of love, the lodging of delight,
The bowre of blisse, the paradice of pleasure,
The sacred harbour of that hevenly spright,
How was I ravisht with your lovely sight,
And my frayle thoughts too rashly led astray,
Whiles diving deepe through amorous insight,
On the sweet spoyle of beautie they did pray,
And twixt her paps, like early fruit in May,
Whose harvest seemd to hasten now apace,
They loosely did theyr wanton winges display,
And there to rest themselves did boldly place.
  Sweet thoughts! I envy your so happy rest,
  Which oft I wisht, yet never was so blest.

LXXVII

Was it a dreame, or did I see it playne?
A goodly table of pure yvory,
All spred with juncats fit to entertayne
The greatest prince with pompous roialty:
Mongst which, there in a silver dish did ly
Two golden apples of unvalewd price,
Far passing those which Hercules came by,
Or those which Atalanta did entice;
Exceeding sweet, yet voyd of sinfull vice;
That many sought, yet none could ever taste;
Sweet fruit of pleasure, brought from Paradice
By Love himselfe, and in his garden plaste.
  Her brest that table was, so richly spredd;
  My thoughts the guests, which would thereon have
                        fedd.

LXXVIII

Lackyng my Love, I go from place to place,
Lyke a young fawne that late hath lost the hynd,
And seeke each where where last I sawe her face,
Whose ymage yet I carry fresh in mynd.
I seeke the fields with her late footing synd;
I seeke her bowre with her late presence deckt;
Yet nor in field nor bowre I can her fynd,
Yet field and bowre are full of her aspect.
But when myne eyes I therunto direct,
They ydly back return to me agayne;
And when I hope to see theyr trew obiect,
I fynd my self but fed with fancies vayne.
   Cease then, myne eyes, to seeke her selfe to see,
   And let my thoughts behold her selfe in mee.

LXXIX

Men call you fayre, and you doe credit it,
For that your selfe ye daily such doe see:
But the trew fayre, that is the gentle wit
And vertuous mind, is much more praysd of me.
For all the rest, how ever fayre it be,
Shall turne to nought and lose that glorious hew;
But onely that is permanent, and free
From frayle corruption that doth flesh ensew.
That is true beautie: that doth argue you
To be divine, and born of heavenly seed,
Deriv'd from that fayre Spirit from whom all true
And perfect beauty did at first proceed.
  He only fayre, and what he fayre hath made;
  All other fayre, lyke flowres, untymely fade.

LXXXX

After so long a race as I have run
Through Faery land, which those six books compile,
Give leave to rest me being half foredonne,
And gather to my selfe new breath awhile.
Then, as a steed refreshed after toyle,
Out of my prison I will break anew,
And stoutly will that second work assoyle,
With strong endevour and attention dew.
Till then give leave to me in pleasant mew
To sport my Muse, and sing my Loves sweet praise,
The contemplation of whose heavenly hew
My spirit to an higher pitch will rayse.
   But let her prayses yet be low and meane,
   Fit for the handmayd of the Faery Queene.

LXXXI

Fayre is my Love, when her fayre golden haires
With the loose wynd ye waving chance to marke;
Fayre, when the rose in her red cheekes appeares,
Or in her eyes the fyre of love does sparke;
Fayre, when her brest, lyke a rich laden barke,
With pretious merchandize she forth doth lay;
Fayre, when that cloud of pryde, which oft doth dark
Her goodly light, with smiles she drives away.
But fayrest she, when so she doth display
The gate with pearles and rubyes richly dight,
Throgh which her words so wise do make their way,
To beare the message of her gentle spright.
   The rest be works of Natures wonderment;
   But this the worke of harts astonishment.

LXXXII

Ioy of my life! full oft for loving you
I blesse my lot, that was so lucky placed:
But then the more your owne mishap I rew,
That are so much by so meane love embased.
For had the equall hevens so much you graced
In this as in the rest, ye mote invent
Some hevenly wit, whose verse could have enchased
Your glorious name in golden moniment.
But since ye deignd so goodly to relent
To me your thrall, in whom is little worth,
That little that I am shall all be spent
In setting your immortal prayses forth:
  Whose lofty argument, uplifting me,
  Shall lift you up unto an high degree.

LXXXIII

Let not one sparke of filthy lustfull fyre
Breake out, that may her sacred peace molest;
Ne one light glance of sensuall desyre
Attempt to work her gentle mindes unrest:
But pure affections bred in spotlesse brest,
And modest thoughts breathd from well-tempred
                                        spirits,
Goe visit her in her chaste bowre of rest,
Accompanyde with angelick delightes.
There fill your selfe with those most joyous sights,
The which my selfe could never yet attayne:
But speake no word to her of these sad plights,
Which her too constant stiffnesse doth constrayn.
  Onely behold her rare perfection,
  And blesse your fortunes fayre election.

LXXXIV

The world, that cannot deeme of worthy things,
When I doe praise her, say I doe but flatter:
So does the cuckow, when the mavis sings,
Begin his witlesse note apace to clatter.
But they, that skill not of so heavenly matter,
All that they know not, envy or admyre;
Rather then envy, let them wonder at her,
But not to deeme of her desert aspyre.
Deepe in the closet of my parts entyre,
Her worth is written with a golden quill,
That me with heavenly fury doth inspire,
And my glad mouth with her sweet prayses fill:
  Which when as Fame in her shril trump shall
                           thunder,
  Let the world chuse to envy or to wonder.

LXXXV

Venemous tongue, tipt with vile adders sting,
Of that self kynd with which the Furies fell,
Their snaky heads doe combe, from which a spring
Of poysoned words and spightfull speeches well,
Let all the plagues and horrid paines of hell
Upon thee fall for thine accursed hyre,
That with false forged lyes, which thou didst tell.
In my true Love did stirre up coles of yre:
The sparkes whereof let kindle thine own fyre,
And, catching hold on thine own wicked bed,
Consume thee quite, that didst with guile conspire
In my sweet peace such breaches to have bred!
    Shame be thy meed, and mischiefe thy reward,
    Due to thy selfe, that it for me prepard!

LXXXVI

Since I did leave the presence of my Love,
Many long weary dayes I have outworne,
And many nights, that slowly seemd to move
Theyr sad protract from evening untill morn.
For, when as day the heaven doth adorne,
I wish that night the noyous day would end:
And when as night hath us of light forlorne,
I wish that day would shortly reascend.
Thus I the time with expectation spend,
And faine my griefe with chaunges to beguile,
That further seemes his terme still to extend,
And maketh every minute seem a myle.
  So sorrowe still doth seem too long to last;
  But joyous houres do fly away too fast.

LXXXVII

Since I have lackt the comfort of that light
The which was wont to lead my thoughts astray,
I wander as in darknesse of the night,
Affrayd of every dangers least dismay.
Ne ought I see, though in the clearest day,
When others gaze upon theyr shadowes vayne,
But th'donly image of that heavenly ray
Whereof some glance doth in mine eie remayne.
Of which beholding the idaea playne,
Through contemplation of my purest part,
With light thereof I doe my self sustayne,
And thereon feed my love-affamisht hart.
   But with such brightnesse whylest I fill my mind,
   I starve my body, and mine eyes doe blynd.

LXXXVIII

Lyke as the culver on the bared bough
Sits mourning for the absence of her mate,
And in her songs sends many a wishful vow
For his returns, that seemes to linger late,
So I alone, how left disconsolate,
Mourne to my selfe the absence of my Love;
And wandring here and there all desolate,
Seek with my playnts to match that mournful dove
Ne joy of ought that under heaven doth hove,
Can comfort me, but her owne joyous sight,
Whose sweet aspect both God and man can move,
In her unspotted pleasauns to delight.
   Dark is my day, whyles her fayre light I mis,
   And dead my life that wants such lively blis.

The Sonnets

WILLIAM SHAKESPEARE

(1564-1616)

TO. THE .ONLIE . BEGETTER . OF.
THESE . INSVING . SONNETS.
MR. VV. H. ALL .HAPPINESSE.
AND .THAT. ETERNITIE.
PROMISED.

BY.

OVR. EVER-LIVING. POET.

WISHETH.

THE . WELL-WISHING.
ADVENTVRER . IN .
SETTING.
FORTH .

T. T.

1

From fairest creatures we desire increase,
That thereby beauty's rose might never die,
But as the riper should by time decease,
His tender heir might bear his memory:
But thou contracted to thine own bright eyes,
Feed'st thy light's flame with self-substantial fuel,
Making a famine where abundance lies,
Thy self thy foe, to thy sweet self too cruel:
Thou that art now the world's fresh ornament,
And only herald to the gaudy spring,
Within thine own bud buriest thy content,
And, tender churl, mak'st waste in niggarding:
   Pity the world, or else this glutton be,
    To eat the world's due, by the grave and thee.

2

When forty winters shall besiege thy brow,
And dig deep trenches in thy beauty's field,
Thy youth's proud livery so gazed on now,
Will be a totter'd weed of small worth held:
Then being asked, where all thy beauty lies,
Where all the treasure of thy lusty days;
To say, within thine own deep sunken eyes,
Were an all-eating shame, and thriftless praise.
How much more praise deserv'd thy beauty's use,
If thou couldst answer 'This fair child of mine
Shall sum my count, and make my old excuse,'
Proving his beauty by succession thine!
   This were to be new made when thou art old,
   And see thy blood warm when thou feel'st it cold.

3

Look in thy glass and tell the face thou viewest
Now is the time that face should form another;
Whose fresh repair if now thou not renewest,
Thou dost beguile the world, unbless some mother.
For where is she so fair whose unear'd womb
Disdains the tillage of thy husbandry?
Or who is he so fond will be the tomb
Of his self-love, to stop posterity?
Thou art thy mother's glass and she in thee
Calls back the lovely April of her prime;
So thou through windows of thine age shalt see,
Despite of wrinkles this thy golden time.
　But if thou live, remember'd not to be,
　　Die single and thine image dies with thee.

4

Unthrifty loveliness, why dost thou spend
Upon thy self thy beauty's legacy?
Nature's bequest gives nothing, but doth lend,
And being frank she lends to those are free:
Then, beauteous niggard, why dost thou abuse
The bounteous largess given thee to give?
Profitless usurer, why dost thou use
So great a sum of sums, yet canst not live?
For having traffic with thy self alone,
Thou of thy self thy sweet self dost deceive:
Then how when nature calls thee to be gone,
What acceptable audit canst thou leave?
  Thy unused beauty must be tombed with thee,
  Which, used, lives the executor to be.

5

Those hours, that with gentle work did frame
The lovely gaze where every eye doth dwell,
Will play the tyrants to the very same
And that unfair which fairly doth excel;
For never-resting time leads summer on
To hideous winter, and confounds him there;
Sap checked with frost, and lusty leaves quite gone,
Beauty o'er-snowed and bareness every where:
Then were not summer's distillation left,
A liquid prisoner pent in walls of glass,
Beauty's effect with beauty were bereft,
Nor it, nor no remembrance what it was:
  But flowers distill'd, though they with winter meet,
  Leese but their show; their substance still lives
                         sweet.

6

Then let not winter's ragged hand deface,
In thee thy summer, ere thou be distilled:
Make sweet some vial; treasure thou some place
With beauty's treasure ere it be self-killed.
That use is not forbidden usury,
Which happies those that pay the willing loan;
That's for thy self to breed another thee,
Or ten times happier, be it ten for one;
Ten times thy self were happier than thou art,
If ten of thine ten times refigured thee:
Then what could death do if thou shouldst depart,
Leaving thee living in posterity?
  Be not self-willed, for thou art much too fair
  To be death's conquest and make worms thine heir.

7

Lo! in the orient when the gracious light
Lifts up his burning head, each under eye
Doth homage to his new-appearing sight,
Serving with looks his sacred majesty;
And having climbed the steep-up heavenly hill,
Resembling strong youth in his middle age,
Yet mortal looks adore his beauty still,
Attending on his golden pilgrimage:
But when from highmost pitch, with weary car,
Like feeble age, he reeleth from the day,
The eyes, 'fore duteous, now converted are
From his low tract, and look another way:
  So thou, thyself outgoing in thy noon
  Unlooked on diest unless thou get a son.

8

Music to hear, why hear'st thou music sadly?
Sweets with sweets war not, joy delights in joy:
Why lov'st thou that which thou receiv'st not gladly,
Or else receiv'st with pleasure thine annoy?
If the true concord of well-tuned sounds,
By unions married, do offend thine ear,
They do but sweetly chide thee, who confounds
In singleness the parts that thou shouldst bear.
Mark how one string, sweet husband to another,
Strikes each in each by mutual ordering;
Resembling sire and child and happy mother,
Who, all in one, one pleasing note do sing:
   Whose speechless song being many, seeming one,
   Sings this to thee: 'Thou single wilt prove none.'

9

Is it for fear to wet a widow's eye,
That thou consum'st thy self in single life?
Ah! if thou issueless shalt hap to die,
The world will wail thee like a makeless wife;
The world will be thy widow and still weep
That thou no form of thee hast left behind,
When every private widow well may keep
By children's eyes, her husband's shape in mind:
Look what an unthrift in the world doth spend
Shifts but his place, for still the world enjoys it;
But beauty's waste hath in the world an end,
And kept unused the user so destroys it.
    No love toward others in that bosom sits
    That on himself such murd'rous shame commits.

10

For shame deny that thou bear'st love to any,
Who for thy self art so unprovident.
Grant, if thou wilt, thou art beloved of many,
But that thou none lov'st is most evident:
For thou art so possessed with murderous hate,
That 'gainst thy self thou stick'st not to conspire,
Seeking that beauteous roof to ruinate
Which to repair should be thy chief desire.
O! change thy thought, that I may change my mind:
Shall hate be fairer lodged than gentle love?
Be, as thy presence is, gracious and kind,
Or to thyself at least kind-hearted prove:
    Make thee another self for love of me,
    That beauty still may live in thine or thee.

11

As fast as thou shalt wane, so fast thou grow'st
In one of thine, from that which thou departest;
And that fresh blood which youngly thou bestow'st,
Thou mayst call thine when thou from youth
                                       convertest.
Herein lives wisdom, beauty, and increase;
Without this folly, age, and cold decay:
If all were minded so, the times should cease
And threescore year would make the world away.
Let those whom nature hath not made for store,
Harsh, featureless, and rude, barrenly perish:
Look whom she best endow'd, she gave the more;
Which bounteous gift thou shouldst in bounty cherish:
  She carv'd thee for her seal, and meant thereby,
  Thou shouldst print more, not let that copy die.

12

When I do count the clock that tells the time,
And see the brave day sunk in hideous night;
When I behold the violet past prime,
And sable curls, all silvered o'er with white;
When lofty trees I see barren of leaves,
Which erst from heat did canopy the herd,
And summer's green all girded up in sheaves,
Borne on the bier with white and bristly beard,
Then of thy beauty do I question make,
That thou among the wastes of time must go,
Since sweets and beauties do themselves forsake
And die as fast as they see others grow;
 And nothing 'gainst Time's scythe can make defence
 Save breed, to brave him when he takes thee hence.

13

O! that you were your self; but, love, you are
No longer yours, than you your self here live:
Against this coming end you should prepare,
And your sweet semblance to some other give:
So should that beauty which you hold in lease
Find no determination; then you were
Yourself again, after yourself's decease,
When your sweet issue your sweet form should bear.
Who lets so fair a house fall to decay,
Which husbandry in honour might uphold,
Against the stormy gusts of winter's day
And barren rage of death's eternal cold?
  O! none but unthrifts. Dear my love, you know,
  You had a father: let your son say so.

14

Not from the stars do I my judgement pluck;
And yet methinks I have Astronomy,
But not to tell of good or evil luck,
Of plagues, of dearths, or seasons' quality;
Nor can I fortune to brief minutes tell,
Pointing to each his thunder, rain and wind,
Or say with princes if it shall go well
By oft predict that I in heaven find:
But from thine eyes my knowledge I derive,
And, constant stars, in them I read such art
As truth and beauty shall together thrive,
If from thyself, to store thou wouldst convert;
   Or else of thee this I prognosticate:
   Thy end is truth's and beauty's doom and date.

15

When I consider every thing that grows
Holds in perfection but a little moment,
That this huge stage presenteth nought but shows
Whereon the stars in secret influence comment;
When I perceive that men as plants increase,
Cheered and checked even by the self-same sky,
Vaunt in their youthful sap, at height decrease,
And wear their brave state out of memory;
Then the conceit of this inconstant stay
Sets you most rich in youth before my sight,
Where wasteful Time debateth with decay
To change your day of youth to sullied night,
   And all in war with Time for love of you,
   As he takes from you, I engraft you new.

16

But wherefore do not you a mightier way
Make war upon this bloody tyrant, Time?
And fortify your self in your decay
With means more blessed than my barren rhyme?
Now stand you on the top of happy hours,
And many maiden gardens, yet unset,
With virtuous wish would bear you living flowers,
Much liker than your painted counterfeit:
So should the lines of life that life repair,
Which this, Time's pencil, or my pupil pen,
Neither in inward worth nor outward fair,
Can make you live your self in eyes of men.
    To give away yourself, keeps yourself still,
    And you must live, drawn by your own sweet skill.

17

Who will believe my verse in time to come,
If it were fill'd with your most high deserts?
Though yet heaven knows it is but as a tomb
Which hides your life, and shows not half your parts.
If I could write the beauty of your eyes,
And in fresh numbers number all your graces,
The age to come would say 'This poet lies;
Such heavenly touches ne'er touch'd earthly faces.'
So should my papers, yellow'd with their age,
Be scorn'd, like old men of less truth than tongue,
And your true rights be term'd a poet's rage
And stretched metre of an antique song:
  But were some child of yours alive that time,
  You should live twice, in it, and in my rhyme.

18

Shall I compare thee to a summer's day?
Thou art more lovely and more temperate:
Rough winds do shake the darling buds of May,
And summer's lease hath all too short a date:
Sometime too hot the eye of heaven shines,
And often is his gold complexion dimmed,
And every fair from fair sometime declines,
By chance, or nature's changing course untrimmed:
But thy eternal summer shall not fade,
Nor lose possession of that fair thou ow'st,
Nor shall death brag thou wander'st in his shade,
When in eternal lines to time thou grow'st,
  So long as men can breathe, or eyes can see,
  So long lives this, and this gives life to thee.

19

Devouring Time, blunt thou the lion's paws,
And make the earth devour her own sweet brood;
Pluck the keen teeth from the fierce tiger's jaws,
And burn the long-liv'd phoenix, in her blood;
Make glad and sorry seasons as thou fleet'st,
And do whate'er thou wilt, swift-footed Time,
To the wide world and all her fading sweets;
But I forbid thee one most heinous crime:
O! carve not with thy hours my love's fair brow,
Nor draw no lines there with thine antique pen;
Him in thy course untainted do allow
For beauty's pattern to succeeding men.
   Yet, do thy worst old Time: despite thy wrong,
   My love shall in my verse ever live young.

20

A woman's face with nature's own hand painted,
Hast thou, the master mistress of my passion;
A woman's gentle heart, but not acquainted
With shifting change, as is false women's fashion:
An eye more bright than theirs, less false in rolling,
Gilding the object whereupon it gazeth;
A man in hue all hues in his controlling,
Which steals men's eyes and women's souls amazeth.
And for a woman wert thou first created;
Till Nature, as she wrought thee, fell a-doting,
And by addition me of thee defeated,
By adding one thing to my purpose nothing.
    But since she prick'd thee out for women's pleasure,
    Mine be thy love and thy love's use their treasure.

21

So is it not with me as with that Muse,
Stirred by a painted beauty to his verse,
Who heaven itself for ornament doth use
And every fair with his fair doth rehearse,
Making a couplement of proud compare
With sun and moon, with earth and sea's rich gems,
With April's first-born flowers, and all things rare,
That heaven's air in this huge rondure hems.
O! let me, true in love, but truly write,
And then believe me, my love is as fair
As any mother's child, though not so bright
As those gold candles fixed in heaven's air:
   Let them say more that like of hearsay well;
   I will not praise that purpose not to sell.

22

My glass shall not persuade me I am old,
So long as youth and thou are of one date;
But when in thee time's furrows I behold,
Then look I death my days should expiate.
For all that beauty that doth cover thee,
Is but the seemly raiment of my heart,
Which in thy breast doth live, as thine in me:
How can I then be elder than thou art?
O! therefore love, be of thyself so wary
As I, not for myself, but for thee will;
Bearing thy heart, which I will keep so chary
As tender nurse her babe from faring ill.
   Presume not on thy heart when mine is slain,
   Thou gav'st me thine not to give back again.

23

As an unperfect actor on the stage,
Who with his fear is put beside his part,
Or some fierce thing replete with too much rage,
Whose strength's abundance weakens his own heart;
So I, for fear of trust, forget to say
The perfect ceremony of love's rite,
And in mine own love's strength seem to decay,
O'ercharg'd with burthen of mine own love's might.
O! let my looks be then the eloquence
And dumb presagers of my speaking breast,
Who plead for love, and look for recompense,
More than that tongue that more hath more express'd.
  O! learn to read what silent love hath writ:
  To hear with eyes belongs to love's fine wit.

24

Mine eye hath play'd the painter and hath steel'd,
Thy beauty's form in table of my heart;
My body is the frame wherein 'tis held,
And perspective it is best painter's art.
For through the painter must you see his skill,
To find where your true image pictur'd lies,
Which in my bosom's shop is hanging still,
That hath his windows glazed with thine eyes.
Now see what good turns eyes for eyes have done:
Mine eyes have drawn thy shape, and thine for me
Are windows to my breast, where-through the sun
Delights to peep, to gaze therein on thee;
   Yet eyes this cunning want to grace their art,
   They draw but what they see, know not the heart.

25

Let those who are in favour with their stars
Of public honour and proud titles boast,
Whilst I, whom fortune of such triumph bars
Unlook'd for joy in that I honour most.
Great princes' favourites their fair leaves spread
But as the marigold at the sun's eye,
And in themselves their pride lies buried,
For at a frown they in their glory die.
The painful warrior famoused for fight,
After a thousand victories once foiled,
Is from the book of honour razed quite,
And all the rest forgot for which he toiled:
   Then happy I, that love and am beloved,
   Where I may not remove nor be removed.

26

Lord of my love, to whom in vassalage
Thy merit hath my duty strongly knit,
To thee I send this written embassage,
To witness duty, not to show my wit:
Duty so great, which wit so poor as mine
May make seem bare, in wanting words to show it,
But that I hope some good conceit of thine
In thy soul's thought, all naked, will bestow it:
Till whatsoever star that guides my moving,
Points on me graciously with fair aspect,
And puts apparel on my tottered loving,
To show me worthy of thy sweet respect:
   Then may I dare to boast how I do love thee;
   Till then, not show my head where thou mayst prove
me.

27

Weary with toil, I haste me to my bed,
The dear repose for limbs with travel tired;
But then begins a journey in my head
To work my mind, when body's work's expired:
For then my thoughts – from far where I abide –
Intend a zealous pilgrimage to thee,
And keep my drooping eyelids open wide,
Looking on darkness which the blind do see:
Save that my soul's imaginary sight
Presents thy shadow to my sightless view,
Which, like a jewel hung in ghastly night,
Makes black night beauteous, and her old face new.
　　Lo! thus, by day my limbs, by night my mind,
　　For thee, and for myself, no quiet find.

28

How can I then return in happy plight,
That am debarred the benefit of rest?
When day's oppression is not eas'd by night,
But day by night and night by day oppress'd,
And each, though enemies to either's reign,
Do in consent shake hands to torture me,
The one by toil, the other to complain
How far I toil, still farther off from thee.
I tell the day, to please him thou art bright,
And dost him grace when clouds do blot the heaven:
So flatter I the swart-complexion'd night,
When sparkling stars twire not thou gild'st the even.
  But day doth daily draw my sorrows longer,
  And night doth nightly make grief's length seem
                              stronger.

29

When in disgrace with fortune and men's eyes
I all alone beweep my outcast state,
And trouble deaf heaven with my bootless cries,
And look upon myself, and curse my fate,
Wishing me like to one more rich in hope,
Featured like him, like him with friends possessed,
Desiring this man's art, and that man's scope,
With what I most enjoy contented least;
Yet in these thoughts my self almost despising,
Haply I think on thee, and then my state,
Like to the lark at break of day arising
From sullen earth, sings hymns at heaven's gate;
  For thy sweet love remembered such wealth brings
  That then I scorn to change my state with kings.

30

When to the sessions of sweet silent thought
I summon up remembrance of things past,
I sigh the lack of many a thing I sought,
And with old woes new wail my dear time's waste:
Then can I drown an eye, unused to flow,
For precious friends hid in death's dateless night,
And weep afresh love's long since cancell'd woe,
And moan the expense of many a vanish'd sight:
Then can I grieve at grievances foregone,
And heavily from woe to woe tell o'er
The sad account of fore-bemoaned moan,
Which I new pay as if not paid before.
   But if the while I think on thee, dear friend,
   All losses are restor'd and sorrows end.

31

Thy bosom is endeared with all hearts,
Which I by lacking have supposed dead;
And there reigns Love, and all Love's loving parts,
And all those friends which I thought buried.
How many a holy and obsequious tear
Hath dear religious love stol'n from mine eye,
As interest of the dead, which now appear
But things remov'd that hidden in thee lie!
Thou art the grave where buried love doth live,
Hung with the trophies of my lovers gone,
Who all their parts of me to thee did give,
That due of many now is thine alone:
   Their images I lov'd, I view in thee,
   And thou (all they) hast all the all of me.

32

If thou survive my well-contented day,
When that churl Death my bones with dust shall cover
And shalt by fortune once more re-survey
These poor rude lines of thy deceased lover,
Compare them with the bett'ring of the time,
And though they be outstripped by every pen,
Reserve them for my love, not for their rhyme,
Exceeded by the height of happier men.
O! then vouchsafe me but this loving thought:
'Had my friend's Muse grown with this growing age,
A dearer birth than this his love had brought,
To march in ranks of better equipage:
    But since he died and poets better prove,
    Theirs for their style I'll read, his for his love'.

33

Full many a glorious morning have I seen
Flatter the mountain tops with sovereign eye,
Kissing with golden face the meadows green,
Gilding pale streams with heavenly alchemy;
Anon permit the basest clouds to ride
With ugly rack on his celestial face,
And from the forlorn world his visage hide,
Stealing unseen to west with this disgrace:
Even so my sun one early morn did shine,
With all triumphant splendour on my brow;
But out, alack, he was but one hour mine,
The region cloud hath mask'd him from me now.
   Yet him for this my love no whit disdaineth;
   Suns of the world may stain when heaven's sun
                    staineth.

34

Why didst thou promise such a beauteous day,
And make me travel forth without my cloak,
To let base clouds o'ertake me in my way,
Hiding thy bravery in their rotten smoke?
'Tis not enough that through the cloud thou break,
To dry the rain on my storm-beaten face,
For no man well of such a salve can speak,
That heals the wound, and cures not the disgrace:
Nor can thy shame give physic to my grief;
Though thou repent, yet I have still the loss:
The offender's sorrow lends but weak relief
To him that bears the strong offence's cross.
   Ah! but those tears are pearl which thy love sheds,
   And they are rich and ransom all ill deeds.

35

No more be grieved at that which thou hast done:
Roses have thorns, and silver fountains mud:
Clouds and eclipses stain both moon and sun,
And loathsome canker lives in sweetest bud.
All men make faults, and even I in this,
Authorizing thy trespass with compare,
Myself corrupting, salving thy amiss,
Excusing thy sins more than thy sins are;
For to thy sensual fault I bring in sense,
Thy adverse party is thy advocate,
And 'gainst myself a lawful plea commence:
Such civil war is in my love and hate,
   That I an accessary needs must be,
   To that sweet thief which sourly robs from me.

36

Let me confess that we two must be twain,
Although our undivided loves are one:
So shall those blots that do with me remain,
Without thy help, by me be borne alone.
In our two loves there is but one respect,
Though in our lives a separable spite,
Which though it alter not love's sole effect,
Yet doth it steal sweet hours from love's delight.
I may not evermore acknowledge thee,
Lest my bewailed guilt should do thee shame,
Nor thou with public kindness honour me,
Unless thou take that honour from thy name:
  But do not so, I love thee in such sort,
  As thou being mine, mine is thy good report.

37

As a decrepit father takes delight
To see his active child do deeds of youth,
So I, made lame by Fortune's dearest spite,
Take all my comfort of thy worth and truth;
For whether beauty, birth, or wealth, or wit,
Or any of these all, or all, or more,
Entitled in thy parts, do crowned sit,
I make my love engrafted to this store:
So then I am not lame, poor, nor despis'd,
Whilst that this shadow doth such substance give
That I in thy abundance am suffic'd,
And by a part of all thy glory live.
   Look what is best, that best I wish in thee:
   This wish I have; then ten times happy me!

38

How can my muse want subject to invent,
While thou dost breathe, that pour'st into my verse
Thine own sweet argument, too excellent
For every vulgar paper to rehearse?
O! give thy self the thanks, if aught in me
Worthy perusal stand against thy sight;
For who's so dumb that cannot write to thee,
When thou thy self dost give invention light?
Be thou the tenth Muse, ten times more in worth
Than those old nine which rhymers invocate;
And he that calls on thee, let him bring forth
Eternal numbers to outlive long date.
  If my slight muse do please these curious days,
    The pain be mine, but thine shall be the praise.

39

O! how thy worth with manners may I sing,
When thou art all the better part of me?
What can mine own praise to mine own self bring?
And what is't but mine own when I praise thee?
Even for this, let us divided live,
And our dear love lose name of single one,
That by this separation I may give
That due to thee which thou deserv'st alone.
O absence! what a torment wouldst thou prove,
Were it not thy sour leisure gave sweet leave,
To entertain the time with thoughts of love,
Which time and thoughts so sweetly doth deceive,
  And that thou teachest how to make one twain,
  By praising him here who doth hence remain.

40

Take all my loves, my love, yea take them all;
What hast thou then more than thou hadst before?
No love, my love, that thou mayst true love call;
All mine was thine, before thou hadst this more.
Then, if for my love, thou my love receivest,
I cannot blame thee, for my love thou usest;
But yet be blam'd, if thou thy self deceivest
By wilful taste of what thyself refusest.
I do forgive thy robbery, gentle thief,
Although thou steal thee all my poverty:
And yet, love knows it is a greater grief
To bear love's wrong, than hate's known injury.
  Lascivious grace, in whom all ill well shows,
  Kill me with spites yet we must not be foes.

41

Those pretty wrongs that liberty commits,
When I am sometime absent from thy heart,
Thy beauty, and thy years full well befits,
For still temptation follows where thou art.
Gentle thou art, and therefore to be won,
Beauteous thou art, therefore to be assail'd;
And when a woman woos, what woman's son
Will sourly leave her till he have prevail'd?
Ay me! but yet thou might'st my seat forbear,
And chide thy beauty and thy straying youth,
Who lead thee in their riot even there
Where thou art forced to break a twofold truth: –
  Hers by thy beauty tempting her to thee,
  Thine by thy beauty being false to me.

42

That thou hast her it is not all my grief,
And yet it may be said I loved her dearly;
That she hath thee is of my wailing chief,
A loss in love that touches me more nearly.
Loving offenders thus I will excuse ye:
Thou dost love her, because thou know'st I love her;
And for my sake even so doth she abuse me,
Suffering my friend for my sake to approve her.
If I lose thee, my loss is my love's gain,
And losing her, my friend hath found that loss;
Both find each other, and I lose both twain,
And both for my sake lay on me this cross:
  But here's the joy; my friend and I are one;
  Sweet flattery! then she loves but me alone.

43

When most I wink, then do mine eyes best see,
For all the day they view things unrespected;
But when I sleep, in dreams they look on thee,
And darkly bright, are bright in dark directed.
Then thou, whose shadow shadows doth make bright,
How would thy shadow's form form happy show
To the clear day with thy much clearer light,
When to unseeing eyes thy shade shines so!
How would, I say, mine eyes be blessed made
By looking on thee in the living day,
When in dead night thy fair imperfect shade
Through heavy sleep on sightless eyes doth stay!
    All days are nights to see till I see thee,
    And nights bright days when dreams do show thee
                                    me.

44

If the dull substance of my flesh were thought,
Injurious distance should not stop my way;
For then despite of space I would be brought,
From limits far remote, where thou dost stay.
No matter then although my foot did stand
Upon the farthest earth remov'd from thee;
For nimble thought can jump both sea and land,
As soon as think the place where he would be.
But, ah! thought kills me that I am not thought,
To leap large lengths of miles when thou art gone,
But that so much of earth and water wrought,
I must attend time's leisure with my moan;
   Receiving nought by elements so slow
   But heavy tears, badges of either's woe.

45

The other two, slight air, and purging fire
Are both with thee, wherever I abide;
The first my thought, the other my desire,
These present-absent with swift motion slide.
For when these quicker elements are gone
In tender embassy of love to thee,
My life, being made of four, with two alone
Sinks down to death, oppress'd with melancholy;
Until life's composition be recured
By those swift messengers return'd from thee,
Who even but now come back again, assured
Of thy fair health, recounting it to me:
    This told, I joy; but then no longer glad,
    I send them back again, and straight grow sad.

46

Mine eye and heart are at a mortal war,
How to divide the conquest of thy sight;
Mine eye my heart thy picture's sight would bar,
My heart mine eye the freedom of that right.
My heart doth plead that thou in him dost lie,
A closet never pierc'd with crystal eyes,
But the defendant doth that plea deny,
And says in him thy fair appearance lies.
To 'cide this title is impannelled
A quest of thoughts, all tenants to the heart;
And by their verdict is determined
The clear eye's moiety, and the dear heart's part:
  As thus: mine eye's due is thine outward part,
  And my heart's right, thine inward love of heart.

47

Betwixt mine eye and heart a league is took,
And each doth good turns now unto the other:
When that mine eye is famish'd for a look,
Or heart in love with sighs himself doth smother,
With my love's picture then my eye doth feast,
And to the painted banquet bids my heart;
Another time mine eye is my heart's guest,
And in his thoughts of love doth share a part:
So, either by thy picture or my love,
Thy self away, art present still with me;
For thou not farther than my thoughts canst move,
And I am still with them, and they with thee;
  Or, if they sleep, thy picture in my sight
  Awakes my heart, to heart's and eyes' delight.

48

How careful was I when I took my way,
Each trifle under truest bars to thrust,
That to my use it might unused stay
From hands of falsehood, in sure wards of trust!
But thou, to whom my jewels trifles are,
Most worthy comfort, now my greatest grief,
Thou best of dearest, and mine only care,
Art left the prey of every vulgar thief.
Thee have I not lock'd up in any chest,
Save where thou art not, though I feel thou art,
Within the gentle closure of my breast,
From whence at pleasure thou mayst come and part;
  And even thence thou wilt be stol'n I fear,
  For truth proves thievish for a prize so dear.

49

Against that time, if ever that time come,
When I shall see thee frown on my defects,
When as thy love hath cast his utmost sum,
Called to that audit by advis'd respects;
Against that time when thou shalt strangely pass,
And scarcely greet me with that sun, thine eye,
When love, converted from the thing it was,
Shall reasons find of settled gravity;
Against that time do I ensconce me here,
Within the knowledge of mine own desert,
And this my hand, against my self uprear,
To guard the lawful reasons on thy part:
   To leave poor me thou hast the strength of laws,
   Since why to love I can allege no cause.

50

How heavy do I journey on the way,
When what I seek, my weary travel's end,
Doth teach that ease and that repose to say,
'Thus far the miles are measured from thy friend!'
The beast that bears me, tired with my woe,
Plods dully on, to bear that weight in me,
As if by some instinct the wretch did know
His rider lov'd not speed being made from thee.
The bloody spur cannot provoke him on,
That sometimes anger thrusts into his hide,
Which heavily he answers with a groan,
More sharp to me than spurring to his side;
   For that same groan doth put this in my mind,
   My grief lies onward, and my joy behind.

51

Thus can my love excuse the slow offence
Of my dull bearer when from thee I speed:
From where thou art why should I haste me thence?
Till I return, of posting is no need.
O! what excuse will my poor beast then find,
When swift extremity can seem but slow?
Then should I spur, though mounted on the wind,
In winged speed no motion shall I know,
Then can no horse with my desire keep pace.
Therefore desire, (of perfect'st love being made)
Shall neigh, no dull flesh, in his fiery race;
But love, for love, thus shall excuse my jade-
  Since from thee going, he went wilful-slow,
  Towards thee I'll run, and give him leave to go.

52

So am I as the rich, whose blessed key,
Can bring him to his sweet up-locked treasure,
The which he will not every hour survey,
For blunting the fine point of seldom pleasure.
Therefore are feasts so solemn and so rare,
Since, seldom coming in the long year set,
Like stones of worth they thinly placed are,
Or captain jewels in the carcanet.
So is the time that keeps you as my chest,
Or as the wardrobe which the robe doth hide,
To make some special instant special-blest,
By new unfolding his imprison'd pride.
  Blessed are you whose worthiness gives scope,
  Being had, to triumph; being lacked, to hope.

53

What is your substance, whereof are you made,
That millions of strange shadows on you tend?
Since every one hath, every one, one shade,
And you but one, can every shadow lend.
Describe Adonis, and the counterfeit
Is poorly imitated after you;
On Helen's cheek all art of beauty set,
And you in Grecian tires are painted new:
Speak of the spring, and foison of the year,
The one doth shadow of your beauty show,
The other as your bounty doth appear;
And you in every blessed shape we know.
  In all external grace you have some part,
    But you like none, none you, for constant heart.

54

O! how much more doth beauty beauteous seem
By that sweet ornament which truth doth give.
The rose looks fair, but fairer we it deem
For that sweet odour, which doth in it live.
The canker blooms have full as deep a dye
As the perfumed tincture of the roses,
Hang on such thorns, and play as wantonly
When summer's breath their masked buds discloses:
But, for their virtue only is their show,
They live unwoo'd, and unrespected fade;
Die to themselves. Sweet roses do not so;
Of their sweet deaths are sweetest odours made:
  And so of you, beauteous and lovely youth,
  When that shall fade, my verse distills your truth.

55

Not marble, nor the gilded monuments
Of princes, shall outlive this powerful rhyme;
But you shall shine more bright in these contents
Than unswept stone, besmear'd with sluttish time.
When wasteful war shall statues overturn,
And broils root out the work of masonry,
Nor Mars his sword, nor war's quick fire shall burn
The living record of your memory.
'Gainst death, and all oblivious enmity
Shall you pace forth; your praise shall still find room
Even in the eyes of all posterity
That wear this world out to the ending doom.
  So, till the judgment that yourself arise,
    You live in this, and dwell in lovers' eyes.

56

Sweet love, renew thy force; be it not said
Thy edge should blunter be than appetite,
Which but to-day by feeding is allay'd,
To-morrow sharpened in his former might:
So, love, be thou, although to-day thou fill
Thy hungry eyes, even till they wink with fulness,
To-morrow see again, and do not kill
The spirit of love, with a perpetual dulness.
Let this sad interim like the ocean be
Which parts the shore, where two contracted new
Come daily to the banks, that when they see
Return of love, more blest may be the view;
    As call it winter, which being full of care,
    Makes summer's welcome, thrice more wished,
                            more rare.

57

Being your slave what should I do but tend
Upon the hours, and times of your desire?
I have no precious time at all to spend;
Nor services to do, till you require.
Nor dare I chide the world without end hour,
Whilst I, my sovereign, watch the clock for you,
Nor think the bitterness of absence sour,
When you have bid your servant once adieu;
Nor dare I question with my jealous thought
Where you may be, or your affairs suppose,
But, like a sad slave, stay and think of nought
Save, where you are, how happy you make those.
    So true a fool is love, that in your will,
    Though you do anything, he thinks no ill.

58

That god forbid, that made me first your slave,
I should in thought control your times of pleasure,
Or at your hand the account of hours to crave,
Being your vassal, bound to stay your leisure!
O! let me suffer, being at your beck,
The imprison'd absence of your liberty;
And patience, tame to sufferance, bide each check,
Without accusing you of injury.
Be where you list, your charter is so strong
That you yourself may privilege your time
To what you will; to you it doth belong
Yourself to pardon of self-doing crime.
  I am to wait, though waiting so be hell,
  Not blame your pleasure be it ill or well.

59

If there be nothing new, but that which is
Hath been before, how are our brains beguil'd,
Which labouring for invention bear amiss
The second burthen of a former child.
Oh that record could with a backward look,
Even of five hundred courses of the sun,
Show me your image in some antique book,
Since mind at first in character was done,
That I might see what the old world could say
To this composed wonder of your frame;
Whether we are mended, or where better they,
Or whether revolution be the same.
  Oh sure I am the wits of former days,
   To subjects worse have given admiring praise.

60

Like as the waves make towards the pebbled shore,
So do our minutes hasten to their end;
Each changing place with that which goes before,
In sequent toil all forwards do contend.
Nativity, once in the main of light,
Crawls to maturity, wherewith being crowned,
Crooked eclipses 'gainst his glory fight,
And Time that gave doth now his gift confound.
Time doth transfix the flourish set on youth
And delves the parallels in beauty's brow,
Feeds on the rarities of nature's truth,
And nothing stands but for his scythe to mow:
  And yet to times in hope, my verse shall stand
  Praising thy worth, despite his cruel hand.

61

Is it thy will, thy image should keep open
My heavy eyelids to the weary night?
Dost thou desire my slumbers should be broken,
While shadows like to thee do mock my sight?
Is it thy spirit that thou send'st from thee
So far from home into my deeds to pry,
To find out shames and idle hours in me,
The scope and tenor of thy jealousy?
O, no! thy love, though much, is not so great:
It is my love that keeps mine eye awake:
Mine own true love that doth my rest defeat,
To play the watchman ever for thy sake:
    For thee watch I, whilst thou dost wake elsewhere,
    From me far off, with others all too near.

62

Sin of self-love possesseth all mine eye
And all my soul, and all my every part;
And for this sin there is no remedy,
It is so grounded inward in my heart.
Methinks no face so gracious is as mine,
No shape so true, no truth of such account;
And for myself mine own worth do define,
As I all other in all worths surmount.
But when my glass shows me myself indeed
Beated and chopp'd with tanned antiquity,
Mine own self-love quite contrary I read;
Self so self-loving were iniquity.
   'Tis thee, myself, that for myself I praise,
   Painting my age with beauty of thy days.

63

Against my love shall be as I am now,
With Time's injurious hand crush'd and o'erworn;
When hours have drain'd his blood and fill'd his brow
With lines and wrinkles; when his youthful morn
Hath travell'd on to age's steepy night;
And all those beauties whereof now he's king
Are vanishing, or vanished out of sight,
Stealing away the treasure of his spring;
For such a time do I now fortify
Against confounding age's cruel knife,
That he shall never cut from memory
My sweet love's beauty, though my lover's life:
  His beauty shall in these black lines be seen,
  And they shall live, and he in them still green.

64

When I have seen by Time's fell hand defac'd
The rich proud cost of outworn buried age;
When sometime lofty towers I see down-raz'd,
And brass eternal slave to mortal rage;
When I have seen the hungry ocean gain
Advantage on the kingdom of the shore,
And the firm soil win of the watery main,
Increasing store with loss, and loss with store;
When I have seen such interchange of state,
Or state itself confounded to decay;
Ruin hath taught me thus to ruminate
That Time will come and take my love away.
   This thought is as a death which cannot choose
   But weep to have that which it fears to lose.

65

Since brass, nor stone, nor earth, nor boundless sea,
But sad mortality o'ersways their power,
How with this rage shall beauty hold a plea,
Whose action is no stronger than a flower?
O! how shall summer's honey breath hold out,
Against the wrackful siege of battering days,
When rocks impregnable are not so stout,
Nor gates of steel so strong but Time decays?
O fearful meditation! where, alack,
Shall Time's best jewel from Time's chest lie hid?
Or what strong hand can hold his swift foot back?
Or who his spoil of beauty can forbid?
  O! none, unless this miracle have might,
  That in black ink my love may still shine bright.

66

Tired with all these, for restful death I cry,
As to behold desert a beggar born,
And needy nothing trimm'd in jollity,
And purest faith unhappily forsworn,
And gilded honour shamefully misplac'd,
And maiden virtue rudely strumpeted,
And right perfection wrongfully disgrac'd,
And strength by limping sway disabled
And art made tongue-tied by authority,
And folly, doctor-like, controlling skill,
And simple truth miscall'd simplicity,
And captive good attending captain ill:
   Tir'd with all these, from these would I be gone,
   Save that, to die, I leave my love alone.

67

Ah! wherefore with infection should he live,
And with his presence grace impiety,
That sin by him advantage should achieve,
And lace itself with his society?
Why should false painting imitate his cheek,
And steal dead seeming of his living hue?
Why should poor beauty indirectly seek
Roses of shadow, since his rose is true?
Why should he live, now Nature bankrupt is,
Beggar'd of blood to blush through lively veins?
For she hath no exchequer now but his,
And proud of many, lives upon his gains.
  O! him she stores, to show what wealth she had
  In days long since, before these last so bad.

68

Thus is his cheek the map of days outworn,
When beauty lived and died as flowers do now,
Before these bastard signs of fair were born,
Or durst inhabit on a living brow;
Before the golden tresses of the dead,
The right of sepulchres, were shorn away,
To live a second life on second head;
Ere beauty's dead fleece made another gay:
In him those holy antique hours are seen,
Without all ornament, itself and true,
Making no summer of another's green,
Robbing no old to dress his beauty new;
   And him as for a map doth Nature store,
   To show false Art what beauty was of yore.

69

Those parts of thee that the world's eye doth view
Want nothing that the thought of hearts can mend;
All tongues, the voice of souls, give thee that due,
Uttering bare truth, even so as foes commend.
Thy outward thus with outward praise is crown'd;
But those same tongues, that give thee so thine own,
In other accents do this praise confound
By seeing farther than the eye hath shown.
They look into the beauty of thy mind,
And that in guess they measure by thy deeds;
Then, churls, their thoughts, although their eyes were
                              kind,
To thy fair flower add the rank smell of weeds:
  But why thy odour matcheth not thy show,
  The soil is this, that thou dost common grow.

70

That thou art blamed shall not be thy defect,
For slander's mark was ever yet the fair;
The ornament of beauty is suspect,
A crow that flies in heaven's sweetest air.
So thou be good, slander doth but approve
Thy worth the greater being wooed of time;
For canker vice the sweetest buds doth love,
And thou present'st a pure unstained prime.
Thou hast passed by the ambush of young days
Either not assailed, or victor being charged;
Yet this thy praise cannot be so thy praise,
To tie up envy, evermore enlarged,
  If some suspect of ill masked not thy show,
  Then thou alone kingdoms of hearts shouldst owe.

71

No longer mourn for me when I am dead
Than you shall hear the surly sullen bell
Give warning to the world that I am fled
From this vile world with vilest worms to dwell:
Nay, if you read this line, remember not
The hand that writ it, for I love you so,
That I in your sweet thoughts would be forgot,
If thinking on me then should make you woe.
O! if, I say, you look upon this verse,
When I perhaps compounded am with clay,
Do not so much as my poor name rehearse;
But let your love even with my life decay;
    Lest the wise world should look into your moan,
    And mock you with me after I am gone.

72

O! lest the world should task you to recite
What merit lived in me, that you should love
After my death, - dear love, forget me quite,
For you in me can nothing worthy prove.
Unless you would devise some virtuous lie,
To do more for me than mine own desert,
And hang more praise upon deceased I
Than niggard truth would willingly impart:
O! lest your true love may seem false in this
That you for love speak well of me untrue,
My name be buried where my body is,
And live no more to shame nor me nor you.
   For I am shamed by that which I bring forth,
   And so should you, to love things nothing worth.

73

That time of year thou mayst in me behold
When yellow leaves, or none, or few, do hang
Upon those boughs which shake against the cold,
Bare ruined choirs, where late the sweet birds sang.
In me thou see'st the twilight of such day
As after sunset fadeth in the west;
Which by and by black night doth take away,
Death's second self, that seals up all in rest.
In me thou see'st the glowing of such fire,
That on the ashes of his youth doth lie,
As the death-bed, whereon it must expire,
Consum'd with that which it was nourish'd by.
  This thou perceiv'st, which makes thy love more
                        strong,
  To love that well, which thou must leave ere long.

74

But be contented when that fell arrest
Without all bail shall carry me away,
My life hath in this line some interest,
Which for memorial still with thee shall stay.
When thou reviewest this, thou dost review
The very part was consecrate to thee:
The earth can have but earth, which is his due;
My spirit is thine, the better part of me:
So then thou hast but lost the dregs of life,
The prey of worms, my body being dead;
The coward conquest of a wretch's knife,
Too base of thee to be remembered.
   The worth of that is that which it contains,
   And that is this, and this with thee remains.

So are you to my thoughts as food to life,
Or as sweet-season'd showers are to the ground;
And for the peace of you I hold such strife
As 'twixt a miser and his wealth is found.
Now proud as an enjoyer, and anon
Doubting the filching age will steal his treasure;
Now counting best to be with you alone,
Then better'd that the world may see my pleasure:
Sometime all full with feasting on your sight,
And by and by clean starved for a look;
Possessing or pursuing no delight
Save what is had, or must from you be took.
  Thus do I pine and surfeit day by day,
   Or gluttoning on all, or all away.

76

Why is my verse so barren of new pride,
So far from variation or quick change?
Why with the time do I not glance aside
To new-found methods, and to compounds strange?
Why write I still all one, ever the same,
And keep invention in a noted weed,
That every word doth almost tell my name,
Showing their birth, and where they did proceed?
O! know sweet love I always write of you,
And you and love are still my argument;
So all my best is dressing old words new,
Spending again what is already spent:
   For as the sun is daily new and old,
   So is my love still telling what is told.

77

Thy glass will show thee how thy beauties wear,
Thy dial how thy precious minutes waste;
The vacant leaves thy mind's imprint will bear,
And of this book, this learning mayst thou taste.
The wrinkles which thy glass will truly show
Of mouthed graves will give thee memory;
Thou by thy dial's shady stealth mayst know
Time's thievish progress to eternity.
Look what thy memory cannot contain,
Commit to these waste blanks, and thou shalt find
Those children nursed, deliver'd from thy brain,
To take a new acquaintance of thy mind.
  These offices, so oft as thou wilt look,
  Shall profit thee and much enrich thy book.

78

So oft have I invoked thee for my Muse,
And found such fair assistance in my verse
As every alien pen hath got my use
And under thee their poesy disperse.
Thine eyes, that taught the dumb on high to sing
And heavy ignorance aloft to fly,
Have added feathers to the learned's wing
And given grace a double majesty.
Yet be most proud of that which I compile,
Whose influence is thine, and born of thee:
In others' works thou dost but mend the style,
And arts with thy sweet graces graced be;
  But thou art all my art, and dost advance
  As high as learning my rude ignorance.

79

Whilst I alone did call upon thy aid,
My verse alone had all thy gentle grace;
But now my gracious numbers are decay'd,
And my sick Muse doth give an other place.
I grant, sweet love, thy lovely argument
Deserves the travail of a worthier pen;
Yet what of thee thy poet doth invent
He robs thee of, and pays it thee again.
He lends thee virtue, and he stole that word
From thy behaviour; beauty doth he give,
And found it in thy cheek: he can afford
No praise to thee, but what in thee doth live.
   Then thank him not for that which he doth say,
   Since what he owes thee, thou thyself dost pay.

80

O! how I faint when I of you do write,
Knowing a better spirit doth use your name,
And in the praise thereof spends all his might,
To make me tongue-tied speaking of your fame.
But since your worth, wide as the ocean is,
The humble as the proudest sail doth bear,
My saucy bark, inferior far to his,
On your broad main doth wilfully appear.
Your shallowest help will hold me up afloat,
Whilst he upon your soundless deep doth ride;
Or, being wrack'd, I am a worthless boat,
He of tall building, and of goodly pride:
    Then if he thrive and I be cast away,
    The worst was this, my love was my decay.

81

Or I shall live your epitaph to make,
Or you survive when I in earth am rotten,
From hence your memory death cannot take,
Although in me each part will be forgotten.
Your name from hence immortal life shall have,
Though I, once gone, to all the world must die:
The earth can yield me but a common grave,
When you entombed in men's eyes shall lie.
Your monument shall be my gentle verse,
Which eyes not yet created shall o'er-read;
And tongues to be, your being shall rehearse,
When all the breathers of this world are dead;
  You still shall live, such virtue hath my pen,
  Where breath most breathes, even in the mouths of
                    men.

82

I grant thou wert not married to my Muse,
And therefore mayst without attaint o'erlook
The dedicated words which writers use
Of their fair subject, blessing every book.
Thou art as fair in knowledge as in hue,
Finding thy worth a limit past my praise;
And therefore art enforced to seek anew
Some fresher stamp of the time-bettering days.
And do so, love; yet when they have devis'd,
What strained touches rhetoric can lend,
Thou truly fair, wert truly sympathiz'd
In true plain words, by thy true-telling friend;
   And their gross painting might be better usd
   Where cheeks need blood; in thee it is abusd.

83

I never saw that you did painting need,
And therefore to your fair no painting set;
I found, or thought I found, you did exceed
The barren tender of a poet's debt:
And therefore have I slept in your report,
That you yourself, being extant, well might show
How far a modern quill doth come too short,
Speaking of worth, what worth in you doth grow.
This silence for my sin you did impute,
Which shall be most my glory being dumb;
For I impair not beauty being mute,
When others would give life, and bring a tomb.
    There lives more life in one of your fair eyes
    Than both your poets can in praise devise.

84

Who is it that says most, which can say more,
Than this rich praise, that you alone, are you,
In whose confine immured is the store
Which should example where your equal grew?
Lean penury within that pen doth dwell
That to his subject lends not some small glory;
But he that writes of you, if he can tell
That you are you, so dignifies his story.
Let him but copy what in you is writ,
Not making worse what nature made so clear,
And such a counterpart shall fame his wit,
Making his style admired every where.
  You to your beauteous blessings add a curse,
  Being fond on praise, which makes your praises
                             worse.

85

My tongue-tied Muse in manners holds her still,
While comments of your praise richly compiled,
Reserve thy character with golden quill,
And precious phrase by all the Muses filed.
I think good thoughts, whilst others write good words,
And like unlettered clerk still cry 'Amen'
To every hymn that able spirit affords,
In polished form of well-refined pen.
Hearing you praised, I say ''tis so, 'tis true,'
And to the most of praise add something more;
But that is in my thought, whose love to you,
Though words come hindmost, holds his rank before.
  Then others, for the breath of words respect,
  Me for my dumb thoughts, speaking in effect.

86

Was it the proud full sail of his great verse,
Bound for the prize of all too precious you,
That did my ripe thoughts in my brain inhearse,
Making their tomb the womb wherein they grew?
Was it his spirit, by spirits taught to write
Above a mortal pitch, that struck me dead?
No, neither he, nor his compeers by night
Giving him aid, my verse astonished.
He, nor that affable familiar ghost
Which nightly gulls him with intelligence,
As victors of my silence cannot boast;
I was not sick of any fear from thence:
    But when your countenance filled up his line,
    Then lacked I matter; that enfeebled mine.

87

Farewell! thou art too dear for my possessing,
And like enough thou know'st thy estimate,
The charter of thy worth gives thee releasing;
My bonds in thee are all determinate.
For how do I hold thee but by thy granting?
And for that riches where is my deserving?
The cause of this fair gift in me is wanting,
And so my patent back again is swerving.
Thy self thou gavest, thy own worth then not knowing,
Or me to whom thou gav'st it else mistaking;
So thy great gift, upon misprision growing,
Comes home again, on better judgement making.
  Thus have I had thee, as a dream doth flatter,
  In sleep a king, but waking no such matter.

88

When thou shalt be dispos'd to set me light,
And place my merit in the eye of scorn,
Upon thy side, against myself I'll fight,
And prove thee virtuous, though thou art forsworn.
With mine own weakness being best acquainted,
Upon thy part I can set down a story
Of faults concealed, wherein I am attainted;
That thou in losing me shalt win much glory:
And I by this will be a gainer too;
For bending all my loving thoughts on thee,
The injuries that to myself I do,
Doing thee vantage, double-vantage me.
  Such is my love, to thee I so belong,
  That for thy right, myself will bear all wrong.

89

Say that thou didst forsake me for some fault,
And I will comment upon that offence:
Speak of my lameness, and I straight will halt,
Against thy reasons making no defence.
Thou canst not, love, disgrace me half so ill,
To set a form upon desired change,
As I'll myself disgrace; knowing thy will,
I will acquaintance strangle, and look strange;
Be absent from thy walks; and in my tongue
Thy sweet beloved name no more shall dwell,
Lest I, too much profane, should do it wrong,
And haply of our old acquaintance tell.
  For thee, against my self I'll vow debate,
   For I must ne'er love him whom thou dost hate.

Then hate me when thou wilt; if ever, now;
Now, while the world is bent my deeds to cross,
Join with the spite of fortune, make me bow,
And do not drop in for an after-loss:
Ah! do not, when my heart hath 'scaped this sorrow,
Come in the rearward of a conquered woe;
Give not a windy night a rainy morrow,
To linger out a purposed overthrow.
If thou wilt leave me, do not leave me last,
When other petty griefs have done their spite,
But in the onset come: so shall I taste
At first the very worst of fortune's might;
    And other strains of woe, which now seem woe,
    Compared with loss of thee, will not seem so.

91

Some glory in their birth, some in their skill,
Some in their wealth, some in their body's force,
Some in their garments though new-fangled ill;
Some in their hawks and hounds, some in their horse;
And every humour hath his adjunct pleasure,
Wherein it finds a joy above the rest:
But these particulars are not my measure,
All these I better in one general best.
Thy love is better than high birth to me,
Richer than wealth, prouder than garments' cost,
Of more delight than hawks and horses be;
And having thee, of all men's pride I boast:
   Wretched in this alone, that thou mayst take
   All this away, and me most wretched make.

92

But do thy worst to steal thyself away,
For term of life thou art assured mine;
And life no longer than thy love will stay,
For it depends upon that love of thine.
Then need I not to fear the worst of wrongs,
When in the least of them my life hath end.
I see a better state to me belongs
Than that which on thy humour doth depend:
Thou canst not vex me with inconstant mind,
Since that my life on thy revolt doth lie.
O what a happy title do I find,
Happy to have thy love, happy to die!
   But what's so blessed-fair that fears no blot?
   Thou mayst be false, and yet I know it not.

93

So shall I live, supposing thou art true,
Like a deceived husband; so love's face
May still seem love to me, though altered new;
Thy looks with me, thy heart in other place:
For there can live no hatred in thine eye,
Therefore in that I cannot know thy change.
In many's looks, the false heart's history
Is writ in moods, and frowns, and wrinkles strange.
But heaven in thy creation did decree
That in thy face sweet love should ever dwell;
Whate'er thy thoughts, or thy heart's workings be,
Thy looks should nothing thence, but sweetness tell.
 How like Eve's apple doth thy beauty grow,
  If thy sweet virtue answer not thy show!

94

They that have power to hurt, and will do none,
That do not do the thing they most do show,
Who, moving others, are themselves as stone,
Unmoved, cold, and to temptation slow;
They rightly do inherit heaven's graces,
And husband nature's riches from expense;
They are the lords and owners of their faces,
Others, but stewards of their excellence.
The summer's flower is to the summer sweet,
Though to itself, it only live and die,
But if that flower with base infection meet,
The basest weed outbraves his dignity:
   For sweetest things turn sourest by their deeds;
   Lilies that fester, smell far worse than weeds.

95

How sweet and lovely dost thou make the shame
Which, like a canker in the fragrant rose,
Doth spot the beauty of thy budding name!
O! in what sweets dost thou thy sins enclose.
That tongue that tells the story of thy days,
Making lascivious comments on thy sport,
Cannot dispraise, but in a kind of praise;
Naming thy name blesses an ill report.
O! what a mansion have those vices got
Which for their habitation chose out thee,
Where beauty's veil doth cover every blot
And all things turns to fair that eyes can see!
   Take heed, dear heart, of this large privilege;
   The hardest knife ill-used doth lose his edge.

96

Some say thy fault is youth, some wantonness;
Some say thy grace is youth and gentle sport;
Both grace and faults are lov'd of more and less:
Thou mak'st faults graces that to thee resort.
As on the finger of a throned queen
The basest jewel will be well esteem'd,
So are those errors that in thee are seen
To truths translated, and for true things deem'd.
How many lambs might the stern wolf betray,
If like a lamb he could his looks translate!
How many gazers mightst thou lead away,
If thou wouldst use the strength of all thy state!
   But do not so; I love thee in such sort,
    As, thou being mine, mine is thy good report.

97

How like a winter hath my absence been
From thee, the pleasure of the fleeting year!
What freezings have I felt, what dark days seen!
What old December's bareness everywhere!
And yet this time removed was summer's time;
The teeming autumn, big with rich increase,
Bearing the wanton burden of the prime,
Like widow'd wombs after their lords' decease:
Yet this abundant issue seemed to me
But hope of orphans, and unfathered fruit;
For summer and his pleasures wait on thee,
And, thou away, the very birds are mute:
  Or, if they sing, 'tis with so dull a cheer,
  That leaves look pale, dreading the winter's near.

98

From you have I been absent in the spring,
When proud-pied April, dress'd in all his trim,
Hath put a spirit of youth in every thing,
That heavy Saturn laughed and leapt with him.
Yet nor the lays of birds, nor the sweet smell
Of different flowers in odour and in hue,
Could make me any summer's story tell,
Or from their proud lap pluck them where they grew:
Nor did I wonder at the lily's white,
Nor praise the deep vermilion in the rose;
They were but sweet, but figures of delight,
Drawn after you, you pattern of all those.
   Yet seemed it winter still, and you away,
   As with your shadow I with these did play.

99

The forward violet thus did I chide:
Sweet thief, whence didst thou steal thy sweet that
                                          smells,
If not from my love's breath? The purple pride
Which on thy soft cheek for complexion dwells
In my love's veins thou hast too grossly dy'd.
The lily I condemned for thy hand,
And buds of marjoram had stol'n thy hair;
The roses fearfully on thorns did stand,
One blushing shame, another white despair;
A third, nor red nor white, had stol'n of both,
And to his robbery had annex'd thy breath;
But, for his theft, in pride of all his growth
A vengeful canker eat him up to death.
    More flowers I noted, yet I none could see,
    But sweet, or colour it had stol'n from thee.

100

Where art thou Muse that thou forget'st so long,
To speak of that which gives thee all thy might?
Spend'st thou thy fury on some worthless song,
Darkening thy power to lend base subjects light?
Return forgetful Muse, and straight redeem,
In gentle numbers time so idly spent;
Sing to the ear that doth thy lays esteem
And gives thy pen both skill and argument.
Rise, resty Muse, my love's sweet face survey,
If Time have any wrinkle graven there;
If any, be a satire to decay,
And make time's spoils despised every where.
   Give my love fame faster than Time wastes life,
   So thou prevent'st his scythe and crooked knife.

101

O truant Muse what shall be thy amends
For thy neglect of truth in beauty dyed?
Both truth and beauty on my love depends;
So dost thou too, and therein dignified.
Make answer Muse: wilt thou not haply say,
'Truth needs no colour, with his colour fixed;
Beauty no pencil, beauty's truth to lay;
But best is best, if never intermixed'?
Because he needs no praise, wilt thou be dumb?
Excuse not silence so, for't lies in thee
To make him much outlive a gilded tomb
And to be praised of ages yet to be.
   Then do thy office, Muse; I teach thee how
   To make him seem, long hence, as he shows now.

102

My love is strengthened, though more weak in seeming;
I love not less, though less the show appear;
That love is merchandized, whose rich esteeming,
The owner's tongue doth publish every where.
Our love was new, and then but in the spring,
When I was wont to greet it with my lays;
As Philomel in summer's front doth sing,
And stops his pipe in growth of riper days:
Not that the summer is less pleasant now
Than when her mournful hymns did hush the night,
But that wild music burthens every bough,
And sweets grown common lose their dear delight.
   Therefore like her, I sometime hold my tongue:
   Because I would not dull you with my song.

Alack! what poverty my Muse brings forth,
That having such a scope to show her pride,
The argument all bare is of more worth
Than when it hath my added praise beside!
O! blame me not, if I no more can write!
Look in your glass, and there appears a face
That over-goes my blunt invention quite,
Dulling my lines, and doing me disgrace.
Were it not sinful then, striving to mend,
To mar the subject that before was well?
For to no other pass my verses tend
Than of your graces and your gifts to tell;
   And more, much more, than in my verse can sit,
   Your own glass shows you when you look in it.

104

To me, fair friend, you never can be old,
For as you were when first your eye I ey'd,
Such seems your beauty still. Three winters cold,
Have from the forests shook three summers' pride,
Three beauteous springs to yellow autumn turn'd,
In process of the seasons have I seen,
Three April perfumes in three hot Junes burn'd,
Since first I saw you fresh, which yet are green.
Ah! yet doth beauty like a dial-hand,
Steal from his figure, and no pace perceiv'd;
So your sweet hue, which methinks still doth stand,
Hath motion, and mine eye may be deceiv'd:
  For fear of which, hear this thou age unbred:
  Ere you were born was beauty's summer dead.

105

Let not my love be called idolatry,
Nor my beloved as an idol show,
Since all alike my songs and praises be
To one, of one, still such, and ever so.
Kind is my love to-day, to-morrow kind,
Still constant in a wondrous excellence;
Therefore my verse to constancy confined,
One thing expressing, leaves out difference.
Fair, kind, and true, is all my argument,
Fair, kind, and true, varying to other words;
And in this change is my invention spent,
Three themes in one, which wondrous scope affords.
  Fair, kind, and true, have often lived alone,
  Which three till now, never kept seat in one.

When in the chronicle of wasted time
I see descriptions of the fairest wights,
And beauty making beautiful old rhyme,
In praise of ladies dead and lovely knights,
Then, in the blazon of sweet beauty's best,
Of hand, of foot, of lip, of eye, of brow,
I see their antique pen would have express'd
Even such a beauty as you master now.
So all their praises are but prophecies
Of this our time, all you prefiguring;
And for they looked but with divining eyes,
They had not skill enough your worth to sing:
   For we, which now behold these present days,
   Have eyes to wonder, but lack tongues to praise.

107

Not mine own fears, nor the prophetic soul
Of the wide world dreaming on things to come,
Can yet the lease of my true love control,
Supposed as forfeit to a confined doom.
The mortal moon hath her eclipse endured,
And the sad augurs mock their own presage;
Incertainties now crown themselves assured,
And peace proclaims olives of endless age.
Now with the drops of this most balmy time,
My love looks fresh, and Death to me subscribes,
Since, spite of him, I'll live in this poor rhyme,
While he insults o'er dull and speechless tribes:
   And thou in this shalt find thy monument,
    When tyrants' crests and tombs of brass are spent.

108

What's in the brain, that ink may character,
Which hath not figured to thee my true spirit?
What's new to speak, what now to register,
That may express my love, or thy dear merit?
Nothing, sweet boy; but yet, like prayers divine,
I must each day say o'er the very same;
Counting no old thing old, thou mine, I thine,
Even as when first I hallowed thy fair name.
So that eternal love in love's fresh case,
Weighs not the dust and injury of age,
Nor gives to necessary wrinkles place,
But makes antiquity for aye his page;
    Finding the first conceit of love there bred,
    Where time and outward form would show it dead.

109

O! never say that I was false of heart,
Though absence seem'd my flame to qualify,
As easy might I from my self depart
As from my soul which in thy breast doth lie:
That is my home of love: if I have ranged,
Like him that travels, I return again;
Just to the time, not with the time exchanged,
So that myself bring water for my stain.
Never believe though in my nature reigned,
All frailties that besiege all kinds of blood,
That it could so preposterously be stained,
To leave for nothing all thy sum of good;
  For nothing this wide universe I call,
    Save thou, my rose, in it thou art my all.

110

Alas! 'tis true, I have gone here and there,
And made my self a motley to the view,
Gored mine own thoughts, sold cheap what is most
                                                    dear,
Made old offences of affections new;
Most true it is, that I have looked on truth
Askance and strangely; but, by all above,
These blenches gave my heart another youth,
And worse essays proved thee my best of love.
Now all is done, have what shall have no end:
Mine appetite I never more will grind
On newer proof, to try an older friend,
A god in love, to whom I am confined.
    Then give me welcome, next my heaven the best,
    Even to thy pure and most most loving breast.

111

O! for my sake do you with Fortune chide,
The guilty goddess of my harmful deeds,
That did not better for my life provide
Than public means which public manners breeds.
Thence comes it that my name receives a brand,
And almost thence my nature is subdued
To what it works in, like the dyer's hand:
Pity me, then, and wish I were renewed;
Whilst, like a willing patient, I will drink
Potions of eisell 'gainst my strong infection;
No bitterness that I will bitter think,
Nor double penance, to correct correction.
  Pity me then, dear friend, and I assure ye,
  Even that your pity is enough to cure me.

112

Your love and pity doth the impression fill,
Which vulgar scandal stamped upon my brow;
For what care I who calls me well or ill,
So you o'er-green my bad, my good allow?
You are my all-the-world, and I must strive
To know my shames and praises from your tongue;
None else to me, nor I to none alive,
That my steeled sense or changes right or wrong.
In so profound abysm I throw all care
Of others' voices, that my adder's sense
To critic and to flatterer stopped are.
Mark how with my neglect I do dispense:
    You are so strongly in my purpose bred,
    That all the world besides methinks y'are dead.

113

Since I left you, mine eye is in my mind;
And that which governs me to go about
Doth part his function and is partly blind,
Seems seeing, but effectually is out;
For it no form delivers to the heart
Of bird, of flower, or shape which it doth latch:
Of his quick objects hath the mind no part,
Nor his own vision holds what it doth catch;
For if it see the rud'st or gentlest sight,
The most sweet favour or deformed'st creature,
The mountain or the sea, the day or night,
The crow, or dove, it shapes them to your feature.
  Incapable of more, replete with you,
   My most true mind thus maketh mine eye untrue.

114

Or whether doth my mind, being crowned with you,
Drink up the monarch's plague, this flattery?
Or whether shall I say, mine eye saith true,
And that your love taught it this alchemy,
To make of monsters and things indigest
Such cherubins as your sweet self resemble,
Creating every bad a perfect best,
As fast as objects to his beams assemble?
O! 'tis the first, 'tis flattery in my seeing,
And my great mind most kingly drinks it up:
Mine eye well knows what with his gust is 'greeing,
And to his palate doth prepare the cup:
　　If it be poisoned, 'tis the lesser sin
　　That mine eye loves it and doth first begin.

115

Those lines that I before have writ do lie,
Even those that said I could not love you dearer:
Yet then my judgment knew no reason why
My most full flame should afterwards burn clearer.
But reckoning Time, whose million'd accidents
Creep in 'twixt vows, and change decrees of kings,
Tan sacred beauty, blunt the sharp'st intents,
Divert strong minds to the course of altering things;
Alas! why, fearing of Time's tyranny,
Might I not then say, 'Now I love you best,'
When I was certain o'er incertainty,
Crowning the present, doubting of the rest?
　Love is a babe, then might I not say so,
　　To give full growth to that which still doth grow?

116

Let me not to the marriage of true minds
Admit impediments. Love is not love
Which alters when it alteration finds,
Or bends with the remover to remove:
O, no! it is an ever-fixed mark,
That looks on tempests and is never shaken;
It is the star to every wandering bark,
Whose worth's unknown, although his height be taken.
Love's not Time's fool, though rosy lips and cheeks
Within his bending sickle's compass come;
Love alters not with his brief hours and weeks,
But bears it out even to the edge of doom.
  If this be error and upon me proved,
   I never writ, nor no man ever loved.

117

Accuse me thus: that I have scanted all,
Wherein I should your great deserts repay,
Forgot upon your dearest love to call,
Whereto all bonds do tie me day by day;
That I have frequent been with unknown minds,
And given to time your own dear-purchased right;
That I have hoisted sail to all the winds
Which should transport me farthest from your sight.
Book both my wilfulness and errors down,
And on just proof surmise accumulate;
Bring me within the level of your frown,
But shoot not at me in your waken'd hate;
  Since my appeal says I did strive to prove
  The constancy and virtue of your love.

118

Like as, to make our appetite more keen,
With eager compounds we our palate urge;
As, to prevent our maladies unseen,
We sicken to shun sickness when we purge;
Even so, being full of your ne'er-cloying sweetness,
To bitter sauces did I frame my feeding;
And, sick of welfare, found a kind of meetness
To be diseased, ere that there was true needing.
Thus policy in love, to anticipate
The ills that were not, grew to faults assur'd,
And brought to medicine a healthful state
Which, rank of goodness, would by ill be cur'd;
  But thence I learn and find the lesson true,
  Drugs poison him that so fell sick of you.

119

What potions have I drunk of Siren tears,
Distilled from limbecks foul as hell within,
Applying fears to hopes, and hopes to fears,
Still losing when I saw myself to win!
What wretched errors hath my heart committed,
Whilst it hath thought itself so blessed never!
How have mine eyes out of their spheres been fitted,
In the distraction of this madding fever!
O benefit of ill! now I find true
That better is by evil still made better;
And ruined love, when it is built anew,
Grows fairer than at first, more strong, far greater.
  So I return rebuked to my content,
  And gain by ill thrice more than I have spent.

120

That you were once unkind befriends me now,
And for that sorrow, which I then did feel,
Needs must I under my transgression bow,
Unless my nerves were brass or hammer'd steel.
For if you were by my unkindness shaken,
As I by yours, you've passed a hell of time;
And I, a tyrant, have no leisure taken
To weigh how once I suffered in your crime.
O! that our night of woe might have remembered
My deepest sense, how hard true sorrow hits,
And soon to you, as you to me, then tendered
The humble salve, which wounded bosoms fits!
  But that your trespass now becomes a fee;
  Mine ransoms yours, and yours must ransom me.

'Tis better to be vile than vile esteemed,
When not to be receives reproach of being;
And the just pleasure lost, which is so deemed
Not by our feeling, but by others' seeing:
For why should others' false adulterate eyes
Give salutation to my sportive blood?
Or on my frailties why are frailer spies,
Which in their wills count bad what I think good?
No, I am that I am, and they that level
At my abuses reckon up their own:
I may be straight though they themselves be bevel;
By their rank thoughts, my deeds must not be shown;
  Unless this general evil they maintain,
    All men are bad and in their badness reign.

122

Thy gift, thy tables, are within my brain
Full charactered with lasting memory,
Which shall above that idle rank remain,
Beyond all date, even to eternity:
Or, at the least, so long as brain and heart
Have faculty by nature to subsist;
Till each to razed oblivion yield his part
Of thee, thy record never can be missed.
That poor retention could not so much hold,
Nor need I tallies thy dear love to score;
Therefore to give them from me was I bold,
To trust those tables that receive thee more:
　　To keep an adjunct to remember thee
　　Were to import forgetfulness in me.

123

No, Time, thou shalt not boast that I do change:
Thy pyramids built up with newer might
To me are nothing novel, nothing strange;
They are but dressings of a former sight.
Our dates are brief, and therefore we admire
What thou dost foist upon us that is old;
And rather make them born to our desire
Than think that we before have heard them told.
Thy registers and thee I both defy,
Not wondering at the present nor the past,
For thy records and what we see doth lie,
Made more or less by thy continual haste.
  This I do vow and this shall ever be;
  I will be true despite thy scythe and thee.

124

If my dear love were but the child of state,
It might for Fortune's bastard be unfathered,
As subject to Time's love or to Time's hate,
Weeds among weeds, or flowers with flowers gathered.
No, it was builded far from accident;
It suffers not in smiling pomp, nor falls
Under the blow of thralled discontent,
Whereto the inviting time our fashion calls:
It fears not policy, that heretic,
Which works on leases of short-number'd hours,
But all alone stands hugely politic,
That it nor grows with heat, nor drowns with showers.
   To this I witness call the fools of time,
    Which die for goodness, who have lived for crime.

Were't aught to me I bore the canopy,
With my extern the outward honouring,
Or laid great bases for eternity,
Which proves more short than waste or ruining?
Have I not seen dwellers on form and favour
Lose all and more by paying too much rent
For compound sweet, forgoing simple savour,
Pitiful thrivers, in their gazing spent?
No; let me be obsequious in thy heart,
And take thou my oblation, poor but free,
Which is not mixed with seconds, knows no art,
But mutual render, only me for thee.
   Hence, thou suborned informer! a true soul
   When most impeached stands least in thy control.

126

O thou, my lovely boy, who in thy power
Dost hold Time's fickle glass, his sickle, hour;
Who hast by waning grown, and therein showest
Thy lovers withering, as thy sweet self growest.
If Nature, sovereign mistress over wrack,
As thou goest onwards still will pluck thee back,
She keeps thee to this purpose, that her skill
May time disgrace and wretched minutes kill.
Yet fear her, O thou minion of her pleasure!
She may detain, but not still keep, her treasure:
   Her audit (though delayed) answered must be,
   And her quietus is to render thee.

127

In the old age black was not counted fair,
Or if it were, it bore not beauty's name;
But now is black beauty's successive heir,
And beauty slandered with a bastard shame:
For since each hand hath put on Nature's power,
Fairing the foul with Art's false borrowed face,
Sweet beauty hath no name, no holy bower,
But is profaned, if not lives in disgrace.
Therefore my mistress' eyes are raven black,
Her eyes so suited, and they mourners seem
At such who, not born fair, no beauty lack,
Sland'ring creation with a false esteem:
    Yet so they mourn becoming of their woe,
    That every tongue says beauty should look so.

128

How oft when thou, my music, music play'st,
Upon that blessed wood whose motion sounds
With thy sweet fingers when thou gently sway'st
The wiry concord that mine ear confounds,
Do I envy those jacks that nimble leap,
To kiss the tender inward of thy hand,
Whilst my poor lips which should that harvest reap,
At the wood's boldness by thee blushing stand!
To be so tickled, they would change their state
And situation with those dancing chips,
O'er whom thy fingers walk with gentle gait,
Making dead wood more bless'd than living lips.
    Since saucy jacks so happy are in this,
    Give them thy fingers, me thy lips to kiss.

The expense of spirit in a waste of shame
Is lust in action: and till action, lust
Is perjured, murderous, bloody, full of blame,
Savage, extreme, rude, cruel, not to trust;
Enjoyed no sooner but despised straight;
Past reason hunted; and no sooner had,
Past reason hated, as a swallowed bait,
On purpose laid to make the taker mad.
Mad in pursuit and in possession so;
Had, having, and in quest to have extreme;
A bliss in proof, and proved, a very woe;
Before, a joy proposed; behind a dream.
  All this the world well knows; yet none knows well
  To shun the heaven that leads men to this hell.

130

My mistress' eyes are nothing like the sun;
Coral is far more red, than her lips red:
If snow be white, why then her breasts are dun;
If hairs be wires, black wires grow on her head.
I have seen roses damasked, red and white,
But no such roses see I in her cheeks;
And in some perfumes is there more delight
Than in the breath that from my mistress reeks.
I love to hear her speak, yet well I know
That music hath a far more pleasing sound:
I grant I never saw a goddess go,
My mistress, when she walks, treads on the ground:
   And yet by heaven, I think my love as rare,
   As any she belied with false compare.

Thou art as tyrannous, so as thou art,
As those whose beauties proudly make them cruel;
For well thou know'st to my dear doting heart
Thou art the fairest and most precious jewel.
Yet, in good faith, some say that thee behold,
Thy face hath not the power to make love groan;
To say they err I dare not be so bold,
Although I swear it to myself alone.
And to be sure that is not false I swear,
A thousand groans, but thinking on thy face,
One on another's neck, do witness bear
Thy black is fairest in my judgment's place.
  In nothing art thou black save in thy deeds,
   And thence this slander, as I think, proceeds.

132

Thine eyes I love, and they, as pitying me,
Knowing thy heart torments me with disdain,
Have put on black and loving mourners be,
Looking with pretty ruth upon my pain.
And truly not the morning sun of heaven
Better becomes the grey cheeks of the east,
Nor that full star that ushers in the even,
Doth half that glory to the sober west,
As those two mourning eyes become thy face:
O! let it then as well beseem thy heart
To mourn for me since mourning doth thee grace,
And suit thy pity like in every part.
   Then will I swear beauty herself is black,
   And all they foul that thy complexion lack.

133

Beshrew that heart that makes my heart to groan
For that deep wound it gives my friend and me!
Is't not enough to torture me alone,
But slave to slavery my sweet'st friend must be?
Me from myself thy cruel eye hath taken,
And my next self thou harder hast engrossed:
Of him, myself, and thee I am forsaken;
A torment thrice three-fold thus to be crossed.
Prison my heart in thy steel bosom's ward,
But then my friend's heart let my poor heart bail;
Whoe'er keeps me, let my heart be his guard;
Thou canst not then use rigour in my jail:
  And yet thou wilt; for I, being pent in thee,
  Perforce am thine, and all that is in me.

134

So now I have confessed that he is thine,
And I my self am mortgaged to thy will,
Myself I'll forfeit, so that other mine
Thou wilt restore to be my comfort still:
But thou wilt not, nor he will not be free,
For thou art covetous, and he is kind;
He learned but surety-like to write for me,
Under that bond that him as fast doth bind.
The statute of thy beauty thou wilt take,
Thou usurer, that put'st forth all to use,
And sue a friend came debtor for my sake;
So him I lose through my unkind abuse.
   Him have I lost; thou hast both him and me:
   He pays the whole, and yet am I not free.

135

Whoever hath her wish, thou hast thy Will,
And Will to boot, and Will in over-plus;
More than enough am I that vexed thee still,
To thy sweet will making addition thus.
Wilt thou, whose will is large and spacious,
Not once vouchsafe to hide my will in thine?
Shall will in others seem right gracious,
And in my will no fair acceptance shine?
The sea, all water, yet receives rain still,
And in abundance addeth to his store;
So thou, being rich in Will, add to thy Will
One will of mine, to make thy large will more.
  Let no unkind, no fair beseechers kill;
   Think all but one, and me in that one Will.

136

If thy soul check thee that I come so near,
Swear to thy blind soul that I was thy Will,
And will, thy soul knows, is admitted there;
Thus far for love, my love-suit, sweet, fulfil.
Will, will fulfil the treasure of thy love,
Ay, fill it full with wills, and my will one.
In things of great receipt with ease we prove
Among a number one is reckoned none:
Then in the number let me pass untold,
Though in thy store's account I one must be;
For nothing hold me, so it please thee hold
That nothing me, a something sweet to thee:
   Make but my name thy love, and love that still,
   And then thou lovest me for my name is 'Will.'

Thou blind fool, Love, what dost thou to mine eyes,
That they behold, and see not what they see?
They know what beauty is, see where it lies,
Yet what the best is take the worst to be.
If eyes, corrupt by over-partial looks,
Be anchored in the bay where all men ride,
Why of eyes' falsehood hast thou forged hooks,
Whereto the judgment of my heart is tied?
Why should my heart think that a several plot,
Which my heart knows the wide world's common
                                   place?
Or mine eyes, seeing this, say this is not,
To put fair truth upon so foul a face?
  In things right true my heart and eyes have erred,
  And to this false plague are they now transferred.

138

When my love swears that she is made of truth,
I do believe her though I know she lies,
That she might think me some untutored youth,
Unlearned in the world's false subtleties.
Thus vainly thinking that she thinks me young,
Although she knows my days are past the best,
Simply I credit her false-speaking tongue:
On both sides thus is simple truth suppressed:
But wherefore says she not she is unjust?
And wherefore say not I that I am old?
O! love's best habit is in seeming trust,
And age in love, loves not to have years told:
   Therefore I lie with her, and she with me,
   And in our faults by lies we flattered be.

139

O! call not me to justify the wrong
That thy unkindness lays upon my heart;
Wound me not with thine eye, but with thy tongue:
Use power with power, and slay me not by art,
Tell me thou lov'st elsewhere; but in my sight,
Dear heart, forbear to glance thine eye aside:
What need'st thou wound with cunning, when thy
                                                   might
Is more than my o'erpressed defence can bide?
Let me excuse thee: ah! my love well knows
Her pretty looks have been mine enemies;
And therefore from my face she turns my foes,
That they elsewhere might dart their injuries:
  Yet do not so; but since I am near slain,
  Kill me outright with looks, and rid my pain.

Be wise as thou art cruel; do not press
My tongue-tied patience with too much disdain;
Lest sorrow lend me words, and words express
The manner of my pity-wanting pain.
If I might teach thee wit, better it were,
Though not to love, yet, love to tell me so;
As testy sick men, when their deaths be near,
No news but health from their physicians know;
For, if I should despair, I should grow mad,
And in my madness might speak ill of thee;
Now this ill-wresting world is grown so bad,
Mad slanderers by mad ears believed be.
   That I may not be so, nor thou belied,
   Bear thine eyes straight, though thy proud heart go
                           wide.

141

In faith I do not love thee with mine eyes,
For they in thee a thousand errors note;
But 'tis my heart that loves what they despise,
Who, in despite of view, is pleased to dote.
Nor are mine ears with thy tongue's tune delighted;
Nor tender feeling, to base touches prone,
Nor taste, nor smell, desire to be invited
To any sensual feast with thee alone:
But my five wits nor my five senses can
Dissuade one foolish heart from serving thee,
Who leaves unswayed the likeness of a man,
Thy proud heart's slave and vassal wretch to be:
  Only my plague thus far I count my gain,
  That she that makes me sin awards me pain.

142

Love is my sin, and thy dear virtue hate,
Hate of my sin, grounded on sinful loving:
O! but with mine compare thou thine own state,
And thou shalt find it merits not reproving;
Or, if it do, not from those lips of thine,
That have profaned their scarlet ornaments
And sealed false bonds of love as oft as mine,
Robbed others' beds' revenues of their rents.
Be it lawful I love thee, as thou lov'st those
Whom thine eyes woo as mine importune thee:
Root pity in thy heart, that, when it grows,
Thy pity may deserve to pitied be.
  If thou dost seek to have what thou dost hide,
  By self-example mayst thou be denied!

143

Lo, as a careful housewife runs to catch
One of her feather'd creatures broke away,
Sets down her babe, and makes all swift dispatch
In pursuit of the thing she would have stay;
Whilst her neglected child holds her in chase,
Cries to catch her whose busy care is bent
To follow that which flies before her face,
Not prizing her poor infant's discontent;
So runn'st thou after that which flies from thee,
Whilst I thy babe chase thee afar behind;
But if thou catch thy hope, turn back to me,
And play the mother's part, kiss me, be kind;
    So will I pray that thou mayst have thy 'Will,'
    If thou turn back and my loud crying still.

Two loves I have of comfort and despair,
Which like two spirits do suggest me still:
The better angel is a man right fair,
The worser spirit a woman coloured ill.
To win me soon to hell, my female evil,
Tempteth my better angel from my side,
And would corrupt my saint to be a devil,
Wooing his purity with her foul pride.
And whether that my angel be turned fiend,
Suspect I may, yet not directly tell;
But being both from me, both to each friend,
I guess one angel in another's hell:
   Yet this shall I ne'er know, but live in doubt,
   Till my bad angel fire my good one out.

145

Those lips that Love's own hand did make,
Breathed forth the sound that said 'I hate',
To me that languished for her sake:
But when she saw my woeful state,
Straight in her heart did mercy come,
Chiding that tongue that ever sweet
Was used in giving gentle doom;
And taught it thus anew to greet;
'I hate' she altered with an end,
That followed it as gentle day,
Doth follow night, who like a fiend
From heaven to hell is flown away.
  'I hate', from hate away she threw,
   And saved my life, saying 'not you'.

146

Poor soul, the centre of my sinful earth,
(???) these rebel powers that thee array,
Why dost thou pine within and suffer dearth,
Painting thy outward walls so costly gay?
Why so large cost, having so short a lease,
Dost thou upon thy fading mansion spend?
Shall worms, inheritors of this excess,
Eat up thy charge? Is this thy body's end?
Then soul, live thou upon thy servant's loss,
And let that pine to aggravate thy store;
Buy terms divine in selling hours of dross;
Within be fed, without be rich no more:
   So shall thou feed on Death, that feeds on men,
   And Death once dead, there's no more dying then.

147

My love is as a fever longing still,
For that which longer nurseth the disease;
Feeding on that which doth preserve the ill,
The uncertain sickly appetite to please.
My reason, the physician to my love,
Angry that his prescriptions are not kept,
Hath left me, and I desperate now approve
Desire is death, which physic did except.
Past cure I am, now Reason is past care,
And frantic-mad with evermore unrest;
My thoughts and my discourse as madmen's are,
At random from the truth vainly expressed;
   For I have sworn thee fair, and thought thee bright,
   Who art as black as hell, as dark as night.

148

O me! what eyes hath Love put in my head,
Which have no correspondence with true sight;
Or, if they have, where is my judgment fled,
That censures falsely what they see aright?
If that be fair whereon my false eyes dote,
What means the world to say it is not so?
If it be not, then love doth well denote
Love's eye is not so true as all men's: no,
How can it? O! how can Love's eye be true,
That is so vexed with watching and with tears?
No marvel then, though I mistake my view;
The sun itself sees not, till heaven clears.
   O cunning Love! with tears thou keep'st me blind,
   Lest eyes well-seeing thy foul faults should find.

Canst thou, O cruel! say I love thee not,
When I against myself with thee partake?
Do I not think on thee, when I forgot
Am of my self, all tyrant, for thy sake?
Who hateth thee that I do call my friend,
On whom frown'st thou that I do fawn upon,
Nay, if thou lour'st on me, do I not spend
Revenge upon myself with present moan?
What merit do I in my self respect,
That is so proud thy service to despise,
When all my best doth worship thy defect,
Commanded by the motion of thine eyes?
  But, love, hate on, for now I know thy mind,
  Those that can see thou lov'st, and I am blind.

150

O! from what power hast thou this powerful might,
With insufficiency my heart to sway?
To make me give the lie to my true sight,
And swear that brightness doth not grace the day?
Whence hast thou this becoming of things ill,
That in the very refuse of thy deeds
There is such strength and warrantise of skill,
That, in my mind, thy worst all best exceeds?
Who taught thee how to make me love thee more,
The more I hear and see just cause of hate?
O! though I love what others do abhor,
With others thou shouldst not abhor my state:
  If thy unworthiness raised love in me,
  More worthy I to be beloved of thee.

151

Love is too young to know what conscience is,
Yet who knows not conscience is born of love?
Then, gentle cheater, urge not my amiss,
Lest guilty of my faults thy sweet self prove:
For, thou betraying me, I do betray
My nobler part to my gross body's treason;
My soul doth tell my body that he may
Triumph in love; flesh stays no farther reason,
But rising at thy name doth point out thee,
As his triumphant prize. Proud of this pride,
He is contented thy poor drudge to be,
To stand in thy affairs, fall by thy side.
  No want of conscience hold it that I call
  Her love, for whose dear love I rise and fall.

152

In loving thee thou know'st I am forsworn,
But thou art twice forsworn, to me love swearing;
In act thy bed-vow broke, and new faith torn,
In vowing new hate after new love bearing:
But why of two oaths' breach do I accuse thee,
When I break twenty? I am perjured most;
For all my vows are oaths but to misuse thee,
And all my honest faith in thee is lost:
For I have sworn deep oaths of thy deep kindness,
Oaths of thy love, thy truth, thy constancy;
And, to enlighten thee, gave eyes to blindness,
Or made them swear against the thing they see;
    For I have sworn thee fair; more perjured eye,
    To swear against the truth so foul a lie!

153

Cupid laid by his brand and fell asleep:
A maid of Dian's this advantage found,
And his love-kindling fire did quickly steep
In a cold valley-fountain of that ground;
Which borrowed from this holy fire of Love,
A dateless lively heat, still to endure,
And grew a seething bath, which yet men prove
Against strange maladies a sovereign cure.
But at my mistress' eye Love's brand new-fired,
The boy for trial needs would touch my breast;
I, sick withal, the help of bath desired,
And thither hied, a sad distempered guest,
  But found no cure, the bath for my help lies
  Where Cupid got new fire; my mistress' eyes.

The little Love-god lying once asleep,
Laid by his side his heart-inflaming brand,
Whilst many nymphs that vowed chaste life to keep
Came tripping by; but in her maiden hand
The fairest votary took up that fire
Which many legions of true hearts had warmed;
And so the General of hot desire
Was, sleeping, by a virgin hand disarmed.
This brand she quenched in a cool well by,
Which from Love's fire took heat perpetual,
Growing a bath and healthful remedy,
For men diseased; but I, my mistress' thrall,
  Came there for cure and this by that I prove,
  Love's fire heats water, water cools not love.

FURTHER READING

I. Bell, *et al. A Companion to Shakespeare's Sonnets*, Blackwell, 2006
Sandra Berman. *The Sonnet Over Time*, Chapel Hill, 1988
Harold Bloom, ed. *Shakespeare's Sonnets*, Chelsea House, New York, 1987
S. Booth. *An Essay on Shakespeare's Sonnets*, Yale University Press, 1969
S.C. Campbell. *Only Begotten Sonnets: A Reconstruction of Shakespeare's Sonnets Sequence*, Bell & Hyman, 1978
T.W.H. Crosland. *The English Sonnet*, Hesperides Press, 2006
Reed Way Dasenbrock. *Imitating the Italians: Wyatt, Spenser, Syne, Pound, Joyce,* John Hopkins University Press, Baltimore, 1991
Heather Dubrow. *Captive Victors: Shakespeare's Narrative Poems and Sonnets*, Cornell University Press, Ithaca, 1987
—. *Echoes of Desire: English Petrarchism and Its Counterdiscourses,* Cornell University Press, 1995
Maurice Evans, ed. *Elizabethan Sonnets*, Dent, 1977. 2003
Joel Fineman. *Shakespeare's Perjured Eye: The Invention of Poetic Subjectivity in the Sonnets*, University of California Press, 1988
A. Fowler. *Triumphal Forms: Structural Patterns in Elizabethan Poetry*, Cambridge University Press, 1970
J. Fuller. *The Sonnet* (The Critical Idiom #26), Methuen, 1972
G. Hiller, ed. *Poems of the Elizabethan Age*, Methuen, 1977
Edward Hubler. *The Sense of Shakespeare's Sonnets*, Hill & Wang, New York, 1962
J.B. Leishman. *Themes and Variations in Shakespeare's Sonnets*, Hillary House, New York, 1963
S. Lee, ed. *Elizabethan Sonnets*, Westminster, 1904
J. W. Lever. *The Elizabethan Love Sonnet*, Methuen, 1956
P. Levin. *The Penguin Book of the Sonnet: 500 Years of a Classic Tradition in English*, Penguin, 2001
Arthur Marotti. ""Love is not love": Elizabethan Sonnet Sequences and the Social Order", *English Literary History*, 49, 1982
S. Minta. *Petrarch and Petrarchism*, Manchester University Press, 1980
Kenneth Muir. *Shakespeare's Sonnets*, Allen & Unwin, 1979
S. Regan. *The Sonnet*, Oxford University Press, 2006
G.M. Ridden. *Shakespeare's Sonnets*, Longman, 1982
T. Roche. *Petrarch and the English Sonnet Sequence*, AMS Pres, 1989
Michael R.G. Spiller. *The Development of the Sonnet: An Introduction*, Routledge, 1992
—. *The Sonnet Sequence: A Study of Its Strategies*, Twayne, 1997
. *Early Modern Sonneteers*, Northcote House, Tavistock, 2001
Brent Stirling. *The Shakespeare Sonnet Order: Poems and Groups,*

University of California Press, Berkeley, 1968

Maurice Valency. *In Praise of Love: An Introduction to the Love-Poetry of the Renaissance*, Macmillan, New York, 1961

J.C. Wait. *The Background to Shakespeare's Sonnets*, Chatto & Windus, 1972

James Winny. *The Master-Mistress: A Study of Shakespeare's Sonnets*, Chatto & Windus, 1968

LITERATURE

J.R.R. Tolkien: The Books, The Films, The Whole Cultural Phenomenon
J.R.R. Tolkien: Pocket Guide
Tolkien's Heroic Quest
The *Earthsea* Books of Ursula Le Guin
Beauties, Beasts and Enchantment: Classic French Fairy Tales
German Popular Stories by the Brothers Grimm
Philip Pullman and *His Dark Materials*
Sexing Hardy: Thomas Hardy and Feminism
Thomas Hardy's *Tess of the d'Urbervilles*
Thomas Hardy's *Jude the Obscure*

Thomas Hardy: The Tragic Novels
Love and Tragedy: Thomas Hardy
The Poetry of Landscape in Hardy
Wessex Revisited: Thomas Hardy and John Cowper Powys
Wolfgang Iser: Essays and Interviews
Petrarch, Dante and the Troubadours

Maurice Sendak and the Art of Children's Book Illustration
Andrea Dworkin
Cixous, Irigaray, Kristeva: The *Jouissance* of French Feminism
Julia Kristeva: Art, Love, Melancholy, Philosophy, Semiotics and Psychoanalysis
Hélène Cixous I Love You: The *Jouissance* of Writing

Luce Irigaray: Lips, Kissing, and the Politics of Sexual Difference
Peter Redgrove: Here Comes the Flood
Peter Redgrove: Sex-Magic-Poetry-Cornwall
Lawrence Durrell: Between Love and Death, East and West
Love, Culture & Poetry: Lawrence Durrell

Cavafy: Anatomy of a Soul
German Romantic Poetry: Goethe, Novalis, Heine, Hölderlin
Feminism and Shakespeare
Shakespeare: Love, Poetry & Magic
The Passion of D.H. Lawrence
D.H. Lawrence: Symbolic Landscapes
D.H. Lawrence: Infinite Sensual Violence

Rimbaud: Arthur Rimbaud and the Magic of Poetry
The Ecstasies of John Cowper Powys
Sensualism and Mythology: The Wessex Novels of John Cowper Powys
Amorous Life: John Cowper Powys and the Manifestation of Affectivity (H.W. Fawkner)
Postmodern Powys: New Essays on John Cowper Powys (Joe Boulter)
Rethinking Powys: Critical Essays on John Cowper Powys
Paul Bowles & Bernardo Bertolucci
Rainer Maria Rilke
Joseph Conrad: *Heart of Darkness*
In the Dim Void: Samuel Beckett
Samuel Beckett Goes into the Silence

André Gide: Fiction and Fervour
Jackie Collins and the Blockbuster Novel
Blinded By Her Light: The Love-Poetry of Robert Graves
The Passion of Colours: Travels In Mediterranean Lands
Poetic Forms

POETRY

Ursula Le Guin: Walking In Cornwall
Peter Redgrove: Here Comes The Flood
Peter Redgrove: Sex-Magic-Poetry-Cornwall
Dante: Selections From the Vita Nuova
Petrarch, Dante and the Troubadours
William Shakespeare: Sonnets
William Shakespeare: Complete Poems
Blinded By Her Light: The Love-Poetry of Robert Graves
Emily Dickinson: Selected Poems
Emily Brontë: Poems
Thomas Hardy: Selected Poems
Percy Bysshe Shelley: Poems
John Keats: Selected Poems
Joh n Keats: Poems of 1820
D.H. Lawrence: Selected Poems
Edmund Spenser: Poems
Edmund Spenser: Amoretti
John Donne: Poems
Henry Vaughan: Poems
Sir Thomas Wyatt: Poems
Robert Herrick: Selected Poems
Rilke: Space, Essence and Angels in the Poetry of Rainer Maria Rilke
Rainer Maria Rilke: Selected Poems
Friedrich Hölderlin: Selected Poems
Arseny Tarkovsky: Selected Poems
Arthur Rimbaud: Selected Poems
Arthur Rimbaud: A Season in Hell
Arthur Rimbaud and the Magic of Poetry
Novalis: Hymns To the Night
German Romantic Poetry
Paul Verlaine: Selected Poems
Elizaethan Sonnet Cycles
D.J. Enright: By-Blows
Jeremy Reed: Brigitte's Blue Heart
Jeremy Reed: Claudia Schiffer's Red Shoes
Gorgeous Little Orpheus
Radiance: New Poems
Crescent Moon Book of Nature Poetry
Crescent Moon Book of Love Poetry
Crescent Moon Book of Mystical Poetry
Crescent Moon Book of Elizabethan Love Poetry
Crescent Moon Book of Metaphysical Poetry
Crescent Moon Book of Romantic Poetry
Pagan America: New American Poetry

MEDIA, CINEMA, FEMINISM and CULTURAL STUDIES

J.R.R. Tolkien: The Books, The Films, The Whole Cultural Phenomenon
J.R.R. Tolkien: Pocket Guide
The *Lord of the Rings* Movies: Pocket Guide
The Cinema of Hayao Miyazaki
Hayao Miyazaki: *Princess Mononoke*: Pocket Movie Guide
Hayao Miyazaki: *Spirited Away*: Pocket Movie Guide
Tim Burton
Ken Russell
Ken Russell: *Tommy*: Pocket Movie Guide
The Ghost Dance: The Origins of Religion
The Peyote Cult
Cixous, Irigaray, Kristeva: The *Jouissance* of French Feminism
Julia Kristeva: Art, Love, Melancholy, Philosophy, Semiotics and Psychoanalysis
Luce Irigaray: Lips, Kissing, and the Politics of Sexual Difference
Hélene Cixous I Love You: The *Jouissance* of Writing
Andrea Dworkin
'Cosmo Woman': The World of Women's Magazines
Women in Pop Music
Discovering the Goddess (Geoffrey Ashe)
The Poetry of Cinema
The Sacred Cinema of Andrei Tarkovsky
Andrei Tarkovsky: Pocket Guide
Andrei Tarkovsky: *Mirror*: Pocket Movie Guide
Andrei Tarkovsky: *The Sacrifice*: Pocket Movie Guide
Walerian Borowczyk: Cinema of Erotic Dreams
Jean-Luc Godard: The Passion of Cinema
Jean-Luc Godard: *Hail Mary*: Pocket Movie Guide
Jean-Luc Godard: *Contempt*: Pocket Movie Guide
Jean-Luc Godard: *Pierrot le Fou*: Pocket Movie Guide
John Hughes and Eighties Cinema
Ferris Bueller's Day Off: Pocket Movie Guide
Jean-Luc Godard: Pocket Guide
The Cinema of Richard Linklater
Liv Tyler: Star In Ascendance
Blade Runner and the Films of Philip K. Dick
Paul Bowles and Bernardo Bertolucci
Media Hell: Radio, TV and the Press
An Open Letter to the BBC
Detonation Britain: Nuclear War in the UK
Feminism and Shakespeare
Wild Zones: Pornography, Art and Feminism
Sex in Art: Pornography and Pleasure in Painting and Sculpture
Sexing Hardy: Thomas Hardy and Feminism

In my view *The Light Eternal* is among the very best of all the material I read on Turner. (Douglas Graham, director of the Turner Museum, Denver, Colorado)

The Light Eternal is a model monograph, an exemplary job. The subject matter of the book is beautifully organised and dead on beam. (Lawrence Durrell)

It is amazing for me to see my work treated with such passion and respect. (Andrea Dworkin)

CRESCENT MOON PUBLISHING
P.O. Box 1312, Maidstone, Kent, ME14 5XU, Great Britain. www.crmoon.com

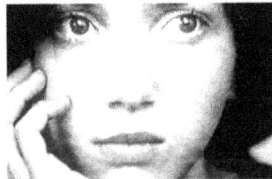

www.ingramcontent.com/pod-product-compliance
Lightning Source LLC
Chambersburg PA
CBHW021151160426
42812CB00078B/662